I0198558

TENNESSEE STORIES

James Dumas

TURNER PUBLISHING COMPANY

Publishers Turner®

200 4th Avenue North, Suite 950
Nashville, TN 37219

445 Park Avenue, 9th Floor
New York, NY 10022

www.turnerpublishing.com

ISBN: 1-56311-344-9
Library of Congress Catalog Card Number:
97-061950

Copyright © 1997
Jim Dumas
Publishing Rights:
Turner Publishing Company
All rights reserved

*This book or any part thereof may not be reproduced without
the written consent of the author or the publishing company.*

*This publication was produced using available material. The publisher
regrets it cannot assume liability for errors or ommissions.*

TABLE OF CONTENTS

About the Author

Jim "Spider" Dumas is widely acclaimed as one of Tennessee's most down to earth writers.

For years, critics ranging from the late Federal Judge Charles Neese of Greeneville to former Tennessee Gov. Ned Ray McWherter, urged Dumas to collect some of his best newspaper feature profiles in a book.

Tennessee Stories is Dumas' second work in fifteen months. His Henry County family history, which highlighted Tennessee's 200th Birthday last year, quickly sold its first printing, and is continuing to sell after its second press run.

Dumas' flair for folksy writing relates to his raising on a family farm in northern Henry County. His common sense good humor that compliments his typical style tells you he did not forget his upbringing.

Dumas, who says he is first a Tennessean, next a Southerner, and finally an American, has entrenched roots, dating to 1821 when Henry County was incorporated. He is a fourth great grandson of the famous David Crockett, and Dumas' third great grandfather, Colonel William A. Tharpe fought in the War of 1812. His great grandfathers, Captain James D. Dumas and W.B. Crutchfield fought for the Confederacy in the War for Southern Independence.

Dumas holds membership in First Families of Tennessee and Lost State of Franklin.

Introduction

Tennessee Stories gives a true life picture of ordinary, down to earth individuals whose good deeds are not likely to make the cover of TIME magazine. But their very presence speaks the same gutsy tongue as the sturdy pioneers who carved Tennessee from the wilderness.

Many of the short stories are revisions of feature profiles I've written in years past as a reporter or publisher of rural newspapers. Others were written in recent months in order to afford geographic balance between East and West Tennessee.

Tennesee Stories presents factual short story biographies about everyday personalities from varied walks of life. There's the brilliant preacher in Middle Tennessee whose talent to build will impress congregations for years to come.

There are Tennessee moonshiners - one retired and one practicing.

Sure to capture the imagination of women is the story about "Mon Cat", who effected one of the state's largest independent telephone systems from scratch.

Audacity compliments two fiery mountaineers in East Tennessee. One was the mayor of Morristown who dared the governor to build a regional prison in his city. Then there was the high sheriff who laid down the law at a state Jaycees convention at Gatlinburg.

If I had to dedicate this book, I suppose it would be to Elizabeth Bagwell, my high school English teacher, who encouraged me to apply whatever talents I had for writing.

And naturally to my mother, Mrs. Billie Williams Dumas, who has waited so long for me to write this book. I also want to thank Gene McCutcheon, whose excellent, expert computer typesetting abilities, expedited the book's progress.

Jim "Spider" Dumas
Paris, Tenn.

Publisher's Message

Turner Publishing Company is proud to recognize the people of Tennessee and help them share their stories in Mr. Dumas' book, *Tennessee Stories*.

Mr. Dumas' vivid description of characters from the Eastern mountains to the Western flatlands creates an accurate, humorous, entertaining, and friendly image of the volunteer state's personality.

This book recognizes the early, proud pioneers who settled the state and the contemporary, innovative leaders who built Tennessee into a prosperous state.

We are honored to present *Tennessee Stories* and to share in Tennessee's rich history.

Sincerely,

Dave Turner
President

Tennessee Stories

Ollie Wofford Left Carnival
for Mountain Home

Sevierville, like other East Ten
nessee towns in the Great Smoky
Mountain range, has witnessed
significant numbers of outsiders
threaten its clannish tradition. In the
years since the county seat of Sevier
County joined Gatlinburg for the al-
mighty tourist dollar, some transplants
— though still eyed with suspicion by
native mountaineers — have received
some degree of acceptance.

Yet, that will be the day when any
non-born person living in Sevierville
will become one of them like Ollie
Wofford.

Ollie came to Sevierville in the
1920s as a carnival worker. After a week the carnival packed up and left on a train,
but with one less hand, because Ollie stayed..

Just why Ollie decided to quit the carnival and adopt Sevierville as his home
was speculated on — even years after his death. Some thought he succumbed to
the beauty of a mountain sunrise.

Possibly, he was wrapped up in the gentle Southern mountain twang which
reminded him of his Eastern Kentucky raisings.

One likely theory is that he was befriended by the friendliness of taxi
drivers Alf and John Newman, known for their grown-up kidding and pranks.
Certainly Ollie was a good-natured — though sometimes a cantankerous butt for
good jokes.

Certainly, Ollie earned his acceptance in a proud mountain clan that

distrusted "furriners" from Northern states and regarded steep-rooted West Tennesseans as "late bloomers."

He became one of them by ringing the bell at First Methodist Church every Sunday morning. For years he volunteered to direct traffic at the county fair and at high school football games.

His circle of friends even saw to it that Ollie was dressed sharply in a blue policeman uniform with badge. It was his favorite garb of all.

There's little doubt that Ollie's political allegiance — if he had one — was checked out by the time the carnival changed trains in Knoxville. Sevier County was the most solid Republican bastion in the nation.

Democrats were so rare that every time a rumor surfaced that a Democrat stepped down from a train — everybody hurried to the station to see what one looked like.

It's no surprise that within days after the carnival left, Ollie was cussing Democrats and furriners from Ohio.

Oh yes ... Ollie could cuss and particularly so if someone bad-mouthed one of his political friends like Judge Ray Reagan. Once he sat in Newman's Cafe and ranted and cussed the morning away because he was told (as a joke) that the young editor of the Sevierville *News Record* was out to beat Judge Reagan in the coming election.

In reality, snow would have come in July before the weekly paper took the slightest stand in a local election. Bill Postlewaite, the gentle-natured Ohio native who owned the newspaper, recognized that election advertising dollars bought newsprint. He also was aware of tempers in heated Sevier County elections.

Well, his son Mark picked a critical time to hurry into Newman's for lunch. The unwitting editor may not have even enjoyed a meal. When Ollie saw Postlewaite, he made a beeline toward the shocked journalist ... shaking both fists and uttering an oath that would have made a sailor blush.

Later, a still shaken Postlewaite returned to his newspaper ... telling aides ... "I just took a verbal whipping from Ollie Wofford and still don't know what I did."

Wofford became a bona fide politician, though ever so unintentional. The Newman brothers were ever circulating petitions and qualifying Ollie for mayor.

If Wofford objected, his "campaign managers" would insist Ollie was the peoples' choice. His backers wrote newspaper ads and speeches. Occasionally, they'd drive Ollie outside Sevierville jurisdiction, like to Pigeon Forge.

Wofford would repeat his campaign platform to crowds and make lavish promises that would have awed past Tennessee governors.

Wofford will guarantee sunshine all year, will put a chicken in every kettle … install street cars … kick Democrats from the state Capitol.

Perhaps the most memorable time of Wofford's political career occurred on a bright sunny day in the 1960s outside the courthouse.

His backers had enticed quite a crowd to have some fun and hear the next mayor.

Wofford was the only candidate challenging Mayor Herb Lawson. The size of the crowd — most lived out of Sevierville — obviously gave him that wining confidence. "Ladies and gentlemen I told you there is always sunshine when old Ollie's here," he started.

At that instant, someone — said to be John Newman — dropped a large balloon filled with water squarely on top of Ollie's head. "You S.O.B.s!" was the abrupt ending to Wofford's most eventful speech.

It's unlikely that Wofford was really worked up over winning, or that Lawson was of losing. After all, everybody was having a little fun, and as always, Wofford relished in the attention. But that's not to say that he didn't eat at his insides when his idol, Judge Reagan, was locked in a hot race.

In the 1974 race for county judge, Reagan looked like a goner, as early counting gave Eugene Huskey, a successful high school basketball coach, an impressive lead.

People recall that Ollie sat, dejected, in the judge's office as if the world was about to end. That gloom turned to party-time for Ollie as the large Seymour precincts voted big for their native son.

The judge's office was a daily stopping place for Wofford, but one day as Ollie was sleeping off a large breakfast of ham and eggs served at Newman's, some pranksters placed an empty fifth of Jim Beam whiskey in his lap. A photographer was summoned and — keeping with standard supermarket tabloid smut — Wofford was a member of the hall of ill fame.

A sad-faced Alf Newman blamed it on Wofford's political enemies. "It looks like they've ruined you and Judge Reagan," kidded Newman.

When Ollie died in the 1970s, his true friends and life's tormentors made sure that Ollie received a proper going away. A large crowd gathered in First Methodist where Ollie, for so many years, had greeted the congregation as he rang the bell.

For a onetime drifting carnival worker who wasn't a Sevierville native, the funeral was beautiful.

Taking a cue from a *News-Record* feature article about Wofford, the preacher — in his sermon — praised Ollie as a man about town.

Oscar Gibson Store in Jeannette, One of the Last Mom and Pops

Were it not for Oscar D. Gibson's Store and the volunteer fire depart ment, the unincorporated town of Jeannette would be off the map. One of the very last of the real country stores, Oscar D. Gibson's is located on Old State Highway 69 — now Jeannette-Holiday Road — in northern Decatur County. Four generations of Gibsons have operated the store since the family moved to North Middle Tennessee from Port Royal, Miss., in the early 1800s.

You might say that Gibson is Jeannette, in that the family owns all the land around. Turns out the community was named after a school teacher who left her mark, although staying only a short duration.

Sherry Briggs, daughter of Oscar Derald Gibson, happened to be visiting her roots recently when the author stopped by the store. Mrs. Briggs, who earned degrees, including a PhD, from Southern universities like Mississippi State and Georgia, recalls childhood memories in a different era when the store meant the world to the rural countryside residents.

The original store was started in 1919 and was later replaced by a much larger brick building, which remains. At one time the store served the needs of the community, dealing in groceries, hardware, furniture, clothes, feed, and farm supplies.

"Sometimes there'd be so many people in the store, you could hardly get about," recalled Sherry. "They'd buy everything from desks to suits, meal, and sugar."

"And others would drink a Grapette or Double Cola and sit around on nail kegs, playing checkers and swapping tales about hunting 'coons and catching catfish in the Tennessee River," interrupted Oscar Gibson.

"The store was just a gathering place where people congregated to catch up on the latest happenings. In the cold of winter, people crowded around the big coal and wood stove in the back of the store ... as you can see it's a big building," he added.

Sherry said one of her fondest memories as a girl was in pumping gas by hand crank in the old round pumps. "I'd get a kick out of pumping gas in somebody's A Model car.

I enjoyed watching the gasoline bubble in that glass enclosure before you'd pumped out a gallon," she said.

Not only did Gibson's Store supply food and household furnishings for the community, it was a means of entertainment and fun. "Lots of weekends there'd be Grand Ole Opry stars like Flatt and Scruggs and Stringbean coming to sing and entertain.

"People gathered in Jeannette from Parsons, Camden and other towns on days like that. That's a part of wholesome rural country life you'll never know again," she deplored.

Sherry also recalls drummers who came by to place orders for goods and wholesale supplies. The drummer would go about the store to check the inventory and recommend what we needed the most, she said.

"'Later the goods would arrive by riverboat, we'd unload our supplies, and sometimes dad or someone would go to Jackson and stock up from a wholesale house," she explained.

The store, Sherry remembers, was fortunate in that nearby farmers raised fresh vegetables such as corn, beans and tomatoes. "We bought many fresh vegetables from our farmers as well as country ham and beef".

Oscar D. Gibson believes that his store is among a dwindling few mom and pop country stores left in Tennessee. "There's us and I think one still in Benton County.

"Things are changing and not always for the good ... you can thank Wal-Mart and greed for that," he said sadly.

Gibson said the biggest insult to consumers has been that the buyer can no longer buy 2 or 3 nails, a small poke of sugar or a half-pound of lard. In the world of Wal-Mart and monopoly, you buy whatever is in the sack, whether you need it or not," he asserted.

"I remember when happy little school kids stopped in and wanted a stick of penny candy because that's all he could afford. He'd be out of luck now."

The Washington government bureaucrats with their asinine regulations may have been a major cause of the disappearing country store, but you wouldn't know that by sizing up the crowd that comes by Gibson's seven days a week.

Farmers and housewives still drop by to buy groceries, household and plumbing supplies. Someone's always pulling up to the gas pumps. And Gibson's is world famous for its extra heaping of fresh ham, cheese, and baloney sandwiches.

Around noon, the place will be packed with truck drivers bringing loads of gravel from nearby Vulcan Materials. As long as the word gets around in the country, Oscar D. Gibson will have his share of the pie and then some.

Davy Crockett's Kin Carry on Legacy

H ow does it feel to be David Crockett's kin?

Since I founded the National Direct Descendants of David Crockett Descendants in August, 1981, I have often been asked two consistent questions by inquisitive newsmen from all over the world.

Make that three ... surely, sensible adults don't believe that Davy killed a bar at the age of three as dramatized in the folk song? Or do they?

At Davy Crockett Birthplace State Park near Limestone, a writer from a Sydney, Australia daily, asked, "How does it feel to be a direct descendant of such a famous person?

My response was that it's not easy. To that, I reflected back to my boyhood years when my mother informed me that David Crockett was her third great-grandfather. That would make me a fourth great-grandson of the famous trail-blazer, Indian fighter, and bear hunter. She also cautioned me about "bragging" to my peers at school. And, as too often — much to a boy's regret — I didn't listen to some well-intended advice.

It wasn't long after that my seventh grade Tennessee history teacher brought up David Crockett in class. Right away, I opened my big mouth and said I was kin to David Crockett. Naturally, that brought laughter and ridicule from my peers. "Sure, I'm kin to George Washington," said a boy who I had just beat in a game of marbles at recess.

"Yeah ... Robert E. Lee was my uncle," teased a freckled-faced girl. She was the All American tom-boy. Even the teacher smirked, but I think her problem was that I had spoiled her lesson plan with my impromptu admission.

But when still another lad rubbed it in, I was ready to change the subject to Shakespeare. "I'm kin to Jessie James." he said, amid much laughter and an angry, redfaced school marm.

Well, the part about America's most famous outlaw baked the cake. As a reporter wrote in his story at one of the organization's conventions a few years ago, I piped down for years about my Crockett kinship.

I don't recall even mentioning it to my shipmates when I was on a warship during the Korean War, nor in college. I know I didn't tell the parents whose daughters I dated.

During my middle age years, I thought about the lifelong research by my great aunt Mildred Tharpe Hope, who had traced David Crockett descendants throughout the United States. At the time, I was part-owner of a weekly newspaper in Pigeon Forge and served as its editor and publisher.

One day I was contacted by a descendant of John Sevier, Tennessee's first governor. The descendants of Sevier were having a family reunion in Gatlinburg … they wanted newspaper coverage.

I was impressed and one of my frequent brainstorms shifted into high gear. I wrote Aunt Mildred who lived in Shelbyville, and told her of my plans. She sent me a list of at least 300 names of Crockett descendants, spread from Maine to California. They were the direct descendants of Crockett's first wife, Polly Finley, and most had roots originating in Paris, Tennessee.

Many descendants who still live in Paris are offsprings of David's and Polly's oldest child, John Wesley Crockett. John Wesley, a lawyer and, like his dad, a former U.S. Congressman, moved to Paris after his famous father settled in northwest Tennessee on the Obion River in Gibson County.

John Wesley married Martha Hamilton, daughter of Judge John Hamilton, Henry County's first circuit judge. Their daughter Elizabeth married into the large and prominent Tharpe family. That's why there are so many of us Crockett direct descendants in Henry County.

I felt strongly that because of Aunt Mildred's lifelong dedication and tireless efforts to Crockett research, the least that I could do was start a living legacy that would recognize her works. So I had a Sevierville lawyer, Circuit Judge Rex Henry Ogle, draw up a charter and bylaws for the National Descendants of David Crockett Association.

The original board of directors, along with myself, were Billie Williams Dumas (my mother), Mildred Tharpe Hope and Virginia McDaniels. Mrs. Dumas remains the only original board member serving.

I estimate that conservatively I have spent $3,000 in personal funds in founding the Crockett family association. The bulk was spent in the first months in which I wrote and telephoned hundreds of persons whose names were on the list compiled by Aunt Mildred.

Despite all my efforts, I succeeded in attracting only seven of Crockett's

direct descendants to the first family reunion at King Arthur Inn at Greeneville, Tennessee in 1984.

However, the nucleus, which included my daughter, Mary Hunt Dumas, couldn't have been better.

Joy Bland and her mother, Sunshine Norwood, came from Paris. Also there were May and Katie Bryers of Chicago, their Tharpe family roots originated in Paris.

That was the beginning of what today is a highly successful organization of about 300 members. Following our second reunion at the Holiday Inn at Greeneville in 1985, we were urged to hold our 1986 convention at the restored David Crockett Hotel in San Antonio, Texas.

Because of the heavy media coverage at the second reunion, many descendants of David's second wife, Elizabeth Patton, had become interested. The result was that the mingling of Tennessee and Texas Crockett cousins mushroomed like wildfire. We agreed to revise the charter so that Tennessee and Texas descendants share the offices and meet every two years at a site in one of the two "T" states.

At the risk of stepping on a Texas cousin's toes, I must confess that Aunt Mildred didn't highly regard the offsprings of Elizabeth Patton's.

There are still copies of a speech in Tennessee museums and libraries she made at a Tennessee Famous Families conference in Lawrenceburg, Tennessee in the 1960s.

Aunt Mildred put down descendants of David and Elizabeth's marriage, passing them off as mere opportunists who had no right to claim the real legend.

Her reasoning was that, had not President Andrew Jackson used his influence to help defeat Congressman Crockett in 1835, he would have never come to Texas to die in the Alamo in the first place.

While that is, of course, true, you had to really know Aunt Mildred to appreciate her comments.

Nevertheless, I have to be proud of the success of the Crockett organization and again, thanks to Aunt Mildred. By the grace of God, she was able to attend that second reunion at Greeneville before she passed on. Maybe it's good there were no Texas cousins at that gathering.

The one negative — to be expected with growing pains — is that too many imposters and selfish opportunists have become fellow travelers. People who are not direct descendants of David Crockett are telling lies to newspapers and television networks.

On the other hand, people who are real descendants are going on TV and taking credit for founding the organization. Perhaps I should send them a bill to help reduce my expenses incurred in the early years.

Finally, there is the fear of the organization's becoming ruled by an oligarchy instead of the Democratic organization intended. Unfortunately, not enough leaders are being encouraged to come forth and get involved.

In the 17 years since the organization started, there have been only four presidents. That is not wholesome for an organization that wants to be eternal.

Then, there is the scenario that so many direct descendants haven't bothered to pay the token dues for membership. That makes you wonder if everybody is proud to be a descendant of such a great man.

Reformed Moonshiner Had Favorite Car

When making and selling moonshine was big in Tennessee, most whiskey runners had a love affair with 1940 Fords. Even in the early 1950s when the illegal trade continued to prosper, souped up '40 Fords were preferred when taking a load of shine from Newport to border states like North Carolina and Virginia.

Moonshiners — some who went on to drive stock cars on NASCAR tracks like Talladega and Charlotte — saw speed as the most likely way to survive in the once highly competitive industry. It wasn't so much as to evade arrest as it was to meet delivery schedules on time. Good drivers found that the 1940 Ford was best when it came to outrunning the law.

Strictly not impressed was reformed moonshiner James Hassell, now a successful contractor and born-again Christian who lives in Centerville.

"In the years I made and ran moonshine, I had lots of good cars," Hassell said. "But none could compare with the 1959 Ford. The reason was that you could load the car down with whiskey and the springs still wouldn't bog down from sheer weight. I had the law behind me many times when I was hauling a 250-gallon load, but I mean that '59 Ford sat up on the road as though it was empty."

Hassell, who served four separate hitches in federal prisons, scoffs at the image of a moonshiner appearing hickish and racing highways at 100 miles-per-hour. "That's the Hollywood image, the Thunder Road and Robert Mitchum movies.

"Only a fool would load 'shine in his car and break speed limits like helter-skelter. He wouldn't last long in the business," said Hassell.

Hassell also said the best way to avoid capture is to act normal.

"When I got ready to haul a load to Nashville or Camden, I'd dress in suit and tie. I'd time my trips to the early morning hours before daylight, so that I'd just be in the normal flow of drivers commuting to work at Nashville plants. And I'd definitely stay within the speed limits.

"There were tricks to the trade ... we used to evade the law, but high speed was so dumb, it's comical."

Hassell was the fifth generation in the family of moonshiners who were raised on Hassell Creek just outside of Centerville in Hickman County. "It was a family tradition and I guess it was my job to keep it going," he mused.

However, time and changing trends have cut into the industry. One of the most obvious factors that have led to a drastic decline in moonshining has been a more liberal outlook by legislators in legalizing the sale of bourbon and other alcohol.

Even as recent as the late 1960s, only five of Tennessee's ninety-five counties had legalized the sale of packaged liquor. The dry counties included Knox County, in which Knoxville — its county seat — is the third largest city in the state.

"Back in the days when the churches and bootleggers joined for opposite reasons and always voted out legal package stores, whiskey-running was a profitable business," asserted Hassell.

"If we worked hard and made a good supply of whiskey, we could take in $700 to $1,000 a week. We paid our boys $50 a day for hauling in the early 1960s. That was good money in those days," he said.

He recalled that in the moonshining heydays, he stilled up to 800 gallons a week on Hassell Creek. "We sold it as fast as we could make it in those days, " he asserted.

Hassell estimates he cleared from about $2 on each gallon of white, which he sold for $4 a gallon. Chartered moonshine, which he stored for six months in empty barrels purchased from Jack Daniels Distillery in Lynchburg, Hassell sold for up to $8 per gallon.

"Hassell Creek was named after my great-great grandpa, Black Jack Hassell," he said. "There were a lot of good springs in the hollers and the local law didn't bother us too much.

"It's funny I guess, but you had friends in the law, even though you were working on the opposite side. I know that Dale Quillen was a revenue agent. He was always after me and my daddy, but we respected him, he was just doing his job.

"Of course we moonshiners paid the law sometimes and even gave them whiskey for special occasions ... they knew we were making it. They knew how hard it was to find jobs in Hickman County. There was only one plant in Centerville and it's too hilly and rocky to farm much."

"I guess Dad taught me all I know about moonshining and when he got caught, I knowed the responsibility of running the business fell on me. After all, we had to pay grocery, automobile and medical bills too."

But Hassell's luck began to change once the federal revenuers got on his trail. "The revenuers finally caught me one day ... I could never prove it, but I'm sure that some other whiskey makers turned me in. It was usually the competitors that turned a moonshiner in, over jealously or plea bargains ... something like that.

"I went up before Judge Frank Gray Jr. in Nashville and I always had respect for the man because he was a straight shooter. The judge gave me two years and they put me in that country club type federal prison at the old Stewart Air Base in Smyrna."

Hassell said that a two-year prison sentence for first violation, was unusual in that it was customary to let first offenders off on probation. "I have no doubt that I wouldn't have served a day if I had plea-bargained and turned another whiskey maker in. But I wasn't born to snitch on somebody else and was ready to serve my time."

Hassell, who recalls that his prison job consisted of mowing grass in the confines of the wall-less 'white collar' prison, was freed after he served four months.

"When I got out, I swore I'd never make another drop of 'shine. But you know? I was back operating another still in two weeks," Hassell laughed.

"Don't ask me why moonshiners like myself couldn't learn their lesson after you get busted. You know good and well the feds are watching you like hawks. I guess you just got brave and the good money in it, it was worth the temptation."

"And for me at least, it was real challenging and we liked to out-do the federal government," he surmised.

Ironically, Hassell credits his experience as head of a moonshine operation with helping him become successful in the legitimate construction business. "I know it sounds funny, but making whiskey was a business. Just like any business, you didn't do too good unless you were a good manager."

In Hassell's world, getting ahead also meant out-foxing the law. "You always had sudden decisions to make. Just as the law wanted to know where I was and what I was doing, I wanted to learn the same about them. I had me a little plane which I learned to junk land in creek bottoms. I used that plane a lot to survey the very people who wanted to lock me up and bust my still," he chuckled.

Hassell scoffed at the widely held theory that people became moonshine suspects when the law learned they had bought large amounts of sugar.

"Sugar was no problem, you could stockpile it by going to wholesale groceries or buying at individual stores two or three times a week."

Hassell, who frequently moved his still around the spring-plentiful hollers, said that he preferred to set up stills near a road or even in barns or vacant houses. A lot of 'shiners thought it was safer to hide by putting stills deep in the woods.

"It was my experience that a hunter or ginseng picker was going to chance up on your still if it was a far piece into the woods. I took my chances close to roads … that way you didn't have so far to tote it to a car."

He also played down the belief that stills were easily detectable because of smoke while cooking. "That could have been a dead give away back during the Depression when you had to burn wood. The modern day moonshiners used butane gas which cuts down the smoke," he explained.

Hassell believes the reason he lasted so long in the moonshine business is because he never drank alcohol. "A good moonshiner didn't make the stuff to drink himself, he made it to sell to others so he could earn his living."

Unlike most in the trade, Hassell didn't judge the quality of the next batch by tasting it. "When you were born and raised into a moonshine family, you knew if your moonshine was fit to drink. I could shake a bottle and look at the bubbles real good and see how clear it looked. I had a lot of pride, I wanted customers to like my product. If they did they'd be back and they'd tell their friends.

"When that pure alcohol starts coming out after heating it at 187 degrees temperature, you can tell if it's good. But it will be potent too, we use to even run our old cars on moonshine," he recalled.

Hassell fared better the second time he appeared before Judge Gray, serving 30 days, although he was placed on four years probation. The third time, however, the judge literally threw the book at the veteran shiner.

"The judge sentenced me to four years to be served at Maxwell Field in Montgomery, Alabama. He also gave me another four years for parole violation.

"They caught me that time in Nashville ... I was driving a big new Cadillac and we had a load right behind it.

"After I served a few months in Montgomery, a federal marshal — who was an old friend — escorted me back to Nashville. They wanted me to plead my Cadillac guilty. When we left for Nashville, I was determined not to surrender the car.

"On the way to Tennessee, the marshal gave me some advice. "He said ... there is a man who wants that Cadillac real bad. What you should do, is plead the car guilty. Otherwise you can count on serving a full four years.

"That was some of the best advice I ever had. I pleaded the car guilty and was free after a year," smiled Hassell.

The third time didn't prove to be the charm for the daring bootlegger either. Soon after leaving Maxwell, he was back in business. This time, the revenuers were determined to end the Hassell illicit trade for good. He was once again apprehended, forced to watch the law dynamite yet another of his stills.

"I had a bunch of stills blown up and not always by the law. There was acid fires and one time I was severely burned and was in Vanderbilt Hospital for about two months," he recalled.

Hassell was arraigned this time, before newly elected federal Judge Tom Wiseman, an unsuccessful candidate for governor in 1974. Hassell was sentenced by Wiseman to three years and given a year's probation. And again, he turned a deaf ear to the feds' attempts to have him rat on other whiskey makers.

Ironically, his staunch refusal to plea bargain by ratting on competitors was to play a huge part in Hassell's success in becoming a reformed citizen.

Finally realizing that he was a marked man in Hickman County, he moved to California to find employment and a new life. It was a time when giant aircraft factories needed a variety of worker help, the sooner the better.

He went to Northrop, the aircraft manufacturer which had a contract with the Air Force to build the stealth bomber. There was no way of hiding his prison record. The FBI had indeed investigated his background, as only the FBI can do. Included in the FBI report, was that Hassell had been steadfast in refusing to identify other moonshiners, knowing full well that it meant additional time behind bars.

That trait was what impressed Northrop officials the most. The stealth bomber was highly confidential. They wanted an inner circle they felt would never betray information about the stealth to Russia. Hassell fit in like Flynn ... suddenly, the reformed hillbilly moonshiner from Hickman County was wearing a white shirt and tie. He was promoted foreman of his shift. What failed to stay confidential around the aircraft plant was Hassell's daring career in moonshining. "I wasn't in California more than a month, until some big wheels at Northrop approached me.

"They wanted to know if I could get them some of that Tennessee moonshine they heard was so good. The next time I went home, I got four gallons of moonshine and four country hams. When I went to Berry Field in Nashville to board a plane back to the west coast, a Colored porter found my suitcases were pretty heavy.

He said. "What you got in there boss?

"I told him ... four country hams and four gallons of white lightening. I handed him a twenty dollar bill. He grinned big, and said 'I'm with you, boss'."

His reputation soon drifted around the elite circles of Hollywood as well. "I ate in Aunt Kissie's Restaurant in Malibu one night, and it's a mighty fancy place. I made them a miniature whiskey still from aluminum foil. As far as I know, it's still displayed on shelves with their other collector's items."

"I liked the job at the aircraft plant real well, I was making good money and it beat running from the law. For a fellow who had a prison record, the people gave me the red carpet treatment."

Would Hassell — if he had life it to do over — choose a life of breaking the law. "There is not any doubt ... given life's same circumstances — I'd follow my moonshining tradition.

"To tell you the truth, the law would be a sight better off today, if all they had to worry about, was busting stills. Moonshiners may have been wrong, but they didn't hurt people.

"For many years now society has been torn apart by heartless drug dealers and dope pushers. Most of them have no respect for human lives — they ruin the lives of young teenagers and show no remorse at all.

"Sure ... I made and run moonshine. But I didn't intentionally hurt no one but myself and my loved ones," said Hassell.

In marked contrast today, he's a God-fearing Christian and member of the Fairview Church of Christ. That rings with a twist of irony too. Hassell recalls that one of his favorite stills was located just behind a church. "The church congregation knew what we was doing behind the church, but never once did they bother us and we never were disrespectful to them."

In Centerville, whose number one daughter is the late Minnie Pearl (Sara Cannon), all is well. The Grinders Switch Motel is located not far from the old Grinders Switch junction on the South Central Tennessee Railroad.

Grinders Switch was the setting where for years, Minnie Pearl fired up Grand Ole Opry crowds with homespun humor about "Brother" and the slow train to Nashville.

Speaking of ironies, the Hassell generations of breaking the law are now very much on the law's side. James Hassell couldn't be prouder of his daughter, Jamie Barnett, fast becoming a veteran Tennessee Highway Patrol officer in Lawrence County.

Old dad must feel lucky he's not hauling contraband these days in expensive automobiles. Trooper Barnett has, in the last year alone, seized 14 cars driven by drunk multiple DUI offenders with revoked licenses. Tougher action to get drunk drivers off roads was approved by the Tennessee General Assembly in 1996. Under the revised DUI law, violators can have their vehicles confiscated.

"Some people in state government wanted to know how one officer could perform so good. She told them she just grew up in that type of life," chuckled Hassell.

And after all the years of daring, tears and heartbreak, something monumental may happen on Hassell Creek. Recently, a bankers' convention was held on the creek where in years past its water was used to manufacture the devil's brew.

Among the guests who walked barefooted in the creek as some kind of hillbilly ritual, were Governor Don Sundquist and Congressman Ed Bryant.

Hassell says he's dead serious about some type of annual festival on Hassell Creek to attract more visitors to Hickman County. And why not? Cosby has its Ramp Festival, Columbia is known for Mule Day and Paris draws thousands of people to the World's Biggest Fish Fry.

Tennessee's Lost County -
Its Tragic Ending

The Courthouse that housed the official records of James County, seat of Tennessee's "lost county" — though now vacant — rests peace fully in a quiet residential neighborhood in old Ooltewah.

Known only by a surprising small number of native Tennesseans, James County opted to declare bankruptcy in 1919.

The county was formed by Act of the State Legislature Jan. 27, 1871 and signed into law three days later by Governor D.W.C. Senter The new county was patterned from lands confiscated from parts of Bradley and Hamilton counties.

2A 88
COUNTY OF JAMES
THE LOST COUNTY OF TENNESSEE
1871-1919

Created out of rivalry of political factions during the reconstruction period following the Civil War, James County consisted of parts of Hamilton and Bradley counties. Plagued by political strife and supported mainly by farmers unable to provide an adequate tax base, its forty-eight year history ended in bankruptcy and its territory became a part of Hamilton County.

TENNESSEE HISTORICAL COMMISSION

The formation of the new county came during post Civil War reconstruction at a time when former Confederates were trying to keep ruthless Northern carpet-baggers at bay.

James County was named in honor of the Rev. Jessie J. James, father of Rep. Elbert Abdiel James, D-Hamilton County who introduced the resolution to the General Assembly, creating the new county.

At the offset, James County was laid off into eight civil districts, eventually growing to as many as ten. After redistricting was ordered by the state legislature in 1912, the civil districts were reduced back to five.

Soon after the districts were determined, an election was held to choose the first county officials. The results were: James Childers, county court clerk; A.L. Stulce, circuit court clerk; Elias Padgett, trustee; John Rustin, register of deeds; and Jessie A. Green, sheriff.

Next came the all important task of choosing a temporary site for government until a permanent location was decided on. The first county court met in Providence Church near Ooltewah.

Leaders in the Northern section of the new county made a strong push for Harrison — the first county seat of Hamilton County. There was logic in that the old courthouse and jail were still intact. Also, Harrison was a key trading site on the Tennessee River.

When it came time to choose the actual county seat, Harrison and Ooltewah were placed in nomination.

The logic in locating the seat in Ooltewah was that it was an important shipping town on the busy Southern Railway.

In bitter balloting, Ooltewah won out , but the process was filled with animosity which would trouble the county throughout is existence.

George Cate was one of the most influential JP's on the James County Court, and was elected several terms as chairman. Other court members in the earlier years, included John Anderson, J.A. Guthrie, Robert Guthrie, and James Rogers.

Court members in later years tried hard to lead the county into solvency following disastrous fires that destroyed two courthouses, intense political conflicts and cash flow woes, included B.F Robinson, chairman, L.A. Parker, Will Tallent, Sam McDaniel and A.P. Gamble.

The county's poor tax base became even more tested by 1911 when Southeast Tennessee counties were asked to pool money for an intercounty road system. There was a drive within the Southeast Tennessee area to build modern roads to make room for new motorized cars. But financially struggling James County remained mired in the horse and buggy days.

County officials such as tax collectors and the sheriff often found it impossible to perform their duties because of muddy trails, hampered by ice and freezing snow.

The deplorable road conditions also played havoc on teachers and students. Mrs. John Moon, the Superintendent of Schools, had to trade her buggy for horseback to perform her responsibilities. Chester Doub, a state education official, required almost two weeks to visit the county's grade schools because of the sad state of roads.

The road conditions, which drained the county's treasury since its inception, proved too much for the county to cope with, without an industrial tax base.

The handwriting was clearly on the wall when it was determined that an $85,000 road appropriation by the county in 1913 was woefully inadequate.

The county's escape from the horse and buggy age was also deemed hopeless when the new Model T Ford horseless carriages found it impossible to navigate the many steep grades in the rural county.

James County was also left behind in the push for free public schools so that all children — regardless of social standing — would have opportunity for at least an eighth grade education.

The county did have some private schools that offered academic excellence for those who could afford them. Among them were Snow Hill Academy and Ooltewah Seminary, founded before the county gained a charter.

Students were also afforded a good education at Male or Female Academy, headed by Professor R.A. Brown. The name was changed to Ooltewah Academy in 1878. The city also had a private secondary school which offered college degrees in the 1880s. In 1891, poorer students were given the opportunity to attend public James High School.

Other institutions of learning which operated in the final years of the impoverished county, included Birchwood Academy, Rutherford Academy, Cheyne Institute and Salem Academy.

In recent years, the building was used for industrial purposes by the Walden Company, which put the building up for sale when the company moved out of state.

The building was purchased by local businessmen, including former State Rep. David Copeland. Copeland, a principal owner, has been negotiating for commercial tenants so that the proud Old South structure will not deteriorate from neglect and sheer loneliness.

Copeland — who was regarded as one of the Tennessee General Assembly's most affective legislators before the Republican quit to make an unsuccessful race for governor in 1994 — would like to see the building's heritage preserved.

One of Copeland's fond memories in the years he served in the legislature is that he sat in the same desk that was assigned early in the century to a House Member representing old James County.

Unfortunately, Copeland has been unsuccessful in getting community involvement so that the old courthouse could become a heritage center or library.

It would seem that the pros far outweigh the cons, in that the building has a unique historical advantage, which cannot be matched anywhere in the state. Nevertheless, a study engineered by Hamilton County brought negative reaction. Two of the excuses given were that public libraries should be located along major highway arteries and that a handicapped access elevator would have to be built.

The local government study committee apparently believed that buying the building for $250,000 and paying for renovations was too costly for a beautiful structure which has a heritage that cannot be bought at any price.

The courthouse, built in 1913, was the third structure — two previous ones burned under suspicious circumstances. The likely deliberate torching of the buildings may well have related to the explosive temper of opposing political factions in the northern and southern sections of James County.

The original courthouse was apparently burned by arsonists in January, 1890. The second courthouse was completed two years later at another site in Ooltewah. Tragedy hit even harder in March, 1913 when the second courthouse burned, destroying the county records.

More industry-minded leaders in the Northern end argued that the county seat should be in Harrison. However, the more dominant rural farmers in the heavily cotton-growing Southern end, insisted on Ooltewah which is located on U.S. Highway 11, about 15 miles east of Chattanooga. Since Ooltewah prevailed, some people have always believed that pro Harrison forces burned the courthouse.

Crack Rogers, whose grandfather, James Rogers Sr. was a justice of peace on the James County Court in the early 1900s, is among Ooltewah history buffs who want to see the courthouse become a heritage center or museum.

"My father, James Rogers Jr., passed away not long ago and he used to talk about growing up in old James County. I'd give anything if we had just wrote down the things daddy used to tell us.

"It's too late now, but it's not too late to preserve forever the history of the lost county. Several years ago, my (Masonic) lodge met in the old courthouse and I remember seeing old James County record books laying around.

"If those books still exist ... just think about how important they would be if the courthouse becomes a heritage center," he said.

When James County surrendered its charter in 1919, its land was given back to Bradley or Hamilton counties.

However, the controversy still lingers on 78 years after the fact. A few years ago, Bradley and Hamilton became embroiled in a legal dispute over an area known as Collegedale, just east of Ooltewah. The courts ruled in Bradley's favor, at least for now.

Lem Ownby, Last Real Mountain Man on Elkmont

My friend, Frank Watson, said he wanted me to meet his cousin, Lem Ownby, who lived several miles up along Jake's Creek. It dawned on me that I had been introduced to Ownby, a 92-year-old blind man, by another of Lem's cousins, Rex Cardwell, about two years before. At that time I had written a feature story on Ownby for the Sevierville *News Record* & *Gatlinburg Press*. Now part owner of a new weekly newspaper, the *Smoky Mountain Star* in Pigeon Forge, I felt a follow-up on this highly unique mountain man wouldn't hurt.

Lem was born 92 years before in the same mountain shack he still called home.

In the years before the creation of the park, Ownby had worked for a giant lumber company which had contracted for timber rights on Elkmont mountain west of Gatlinburg and stretching for miles over Blount County near North Carolina.

After the federal government took over, the once thriving timber camp known as Elkmont gradually begin to decline, but Ownby and a few other timber cutters who had slaved for $1.50 a day in the dangerous life were allowed to remain.

By the time I got around to meeting Lem, he was the only person living in the Elkmont mountains, other than park personnel. In the years since, Ownby had become known as an expert bee raiser. As word spread about Ownby's bees, people came from all over the world to buy his quality wild mountain honey.

If the world had changed within a few miles of Lem's only ever home — which indeed it had — the aging mountaineer still enjoyed the same primitive life as his father. Actually, he had acquired one notable convenience. His son had extended a pipe from the spring about 50 feet away so his father did have running water in his shack.

That pipe which extended water to his back porch for drinking and cooking purposes, seemed to inflate Lem's ego, much like one of today's pampered teens receiving his first color television set.

"You boys are welcome to walk down to the spring to quench the thirst, but you might rather put a glass beneath the pipe," he teased.

Despite his total blindness, Lem possessed an extra sharp perception of hearing that more than made up for the sight handicap.

Lem let us know he was keenly aware that humans were approaching his shack at least 15 minutes before we entered. "One of you stepped on a twig as you started up Jake's Creek. An old bear wouldn't have given that much warning," he said.

Frankly, we were glad not to be one of the numerous black bears around. We learned that Lem was still sore because a bear had bothered his beehives that day before.

"If it's not a bear after my honey, it's wild boars rooting in my garden," complained Ownby.

Woe be the bear who happened to get too close to Lem's domicile when his supply of beef or pork was exhausted. Bear meat has always been a delicacy with hardy mountain men, and Lem was known for making excellent bear stew.

If hungry, though, he'd more than likely shoot a deer who wondered within Ownby's shooting range. Again, with his keen ear, Lem would locate the animal within his sights.

Frank's recollection of the years when trains hauled timber from the lumber camps to the mainline brought an unmistakable tear to the old man's worn face in the shadows of the darkening room.

"When the night air rushes in I can still hear those steam whistles crying," he said,

"I can still see Daddy Bryson's weather-beaten face as he throttled the last train down the grade before day's end.

"I was in that ravine working timber the day Daddy Bryson lost his brakes. There was the dreaded whistle and screaming and mashing of metal when Daddy jumped the track. There was a large hiss of steam … we all knew it was the end for Daddy," said Ownby.

"A lot of good men died and got hurt bad working the timber for a dollar and fifty cents a day. We had our company doctor, Doc B.B. Montgomery, saved a lot of lives and mended people up so they could go on supporting their family.

"The doc did all he could … but now and then as with Daddy Bryson, it had to reach a higher level. None of us were strangers to praying, we went to the little mountain school and learned from the book.

"It was a hard life, but a good life. I don't know why the government took it away from us," he deplored.

As we started to leave, Watson commented on what seemed an unusually large pile of coal near the house.

"Expect a rough winter, Lem," shouted Frank.

"I don't know," answered Ownby. "Roughest winter I lived through was in the winter of 1918. It was the longest cold winter and deepest snow I ever saw.

"A lot of folks died with the flu, a lot of little kids went to early graves. I don't know if this winter will be as rough, but I'll be ready in case," he said.

Claud Miller Buzzed Paris and Scared the Daylights Out of Homefolks

In the closing months of World War II, a Marine airman stepped down from the crack Louisville & Nashville passenger train at the depot in West Paris one midnight.

Claud Miller, raised on a cotton farm west of Paris, didn't have a Purple Heart or rows of Bronze Stars glistening on his dress uniform as did other local sons returning from the Great War. But in his heart, the Good Conduct Medal was proof enough to Miller that he had lived up to his country's expectations.

Yet, the young Marine headed for his parents home on a weekend pass with heavy heart. He wondered if he really ought to be showing off the medal to family and old friends.

His doubts turned to cold reality when he realized that the same familiar friends who had greeted him so warmly on previous visits to his home town were now indifferent and even hostile. Then he heard outrage from citizens who earlier in the day had been frightened and tormented by a low flying military aircraft, which buzzed downtown and peaceful residential sections.

Had the enemy somehow slipped in, though on the verge of losing the war? Or was it a friendly Army Air Force pilot whose mind had suddenly snapped. Was this the beginning of another sneak attack like Pearl Harbor?

Paris, the home of nearby Camp Tyson, was accustomed to troops readying for war and the barrage of balloons that hovered over the camp. Occasionally, a balloon which had been built for protection against enemy air raids broke loose and drifted miles away. By the time the mystery fighter plane raced beneath the courthouse dome and rattled windows and brick chimneys in the business district, the balloons had been phased out and replaced by German prisoners of war.

The presence of German prisoners probably intensified the concern of the population about the plane ... the ladies, children and parents of sons who had gone to war. Had the Germans somehow penetrated United States coastal defenses, bent on freeing their companions in arms?

"I found my old friends and some kinfolks who were hostile and seemed out for blood. "People who I had known and respected as a child seemed unable to control their tempers," recalled Miller.

"They were craving for the blood of anyone who was in that military plane and anyone remotely responsible."

That night Miller wondered why he ever stepped off the Pan American ... why he didn't instead ride the great train miles north.

Miller continued to hear emotional shouts the following day when he strolled through the streets of his native city. By now it had been determined that the low-flying aircraft was a B-24 Marine fighter, based near Newport, Arkansas.

Miller, who had graduated in the 1941 class of E.W. Grove High School before joining the Marines, said nothing as some of the city leaders and elders talked of calling the Pentagon and demanding that "heads roll."

What could he say anyway? Luckily for him, nobody in Paris could suspect that one of the crew members in the joy flying B-24 was the same Claud Miller that now tried to be so understanding and naive.

"I had been on that plane, but I wasn't about to tell a single soul. I practically went out of my mind with worry when I heard a leading public official say he was going to petition Congress for an investigation.

"It had been a good day for us on the B-24 as we hopped the Memphis area. We were getting set to return to base when I halfheartedly joked that we were pretty close to Paris, my hometown. I said. "Wouldn't it be something to fly over my home town?

"Unbeknowing to me, the pilot thought it seemed like a good idea ... having some clean fun before heading in, " recalled Miller.

"The next thing I knew we were down at 3,000 feet and I could see the L & N viaduct out on River Road. Then the pilot dropped lower and lower, skimming between the courthouse and commercial buildings on Poplar Street. If someone had been sitting by a fourth story window in the Commercial Bank building, they could have probably touched us with a broom stick.

"I know, because I was stationed in the upper gun turret as the B-24 flew just over the top of the building. I was horror-struck, I had no idea that the pilot meant to buzz my home town.

"I had the most chilling feeling I ever had or ever will have. I could plainly recognize my daddy, Lee Miller, and my old friends standing in the courthouse lawn. They were frozen in terror, and I feel sure, bracing for falling bombs or machine gun fire.

"Then I got scared. What if my own Daddy looked up and recognized me in that gun turret?

"If things weren't already beyond the point of no return, I had to mention within the pilot's earshot, that my Mother lived on Wynn Street, a few blocks west.

"In a New York instant, the pilot was racing the plane just above the L & N depot and then made a perfect turn south up the middle of Wynn Street.

"I saw dozens of residents running out of houses, as though the end of the world were near. We buzzed just over Nobles Hospital at over 250 miles per hour. I heard later that one of the doctors was so upset and mad that he promised never to rest until he learned who was in the plane.

"It wasn't until we arrived back at the base that we started to sober up to the awful thing we had done. We were frightened to death that the doctor would leave no stone unturned to get to the bottom of what happened.

"The thought was especially provoking to me. I knew that some of those doctors like Arthur Dunlap and Horace McSwain had roots going back to the beginning of Henry County. They had lots of respect."

Miller is convinced that the only reason the crew wasn't court marshaled and given hard labor in federal prison, is that they became blood close. "We were like brothers, we took an oath never to tell anyone, not even our closest relatives."

When the Marine Command reassigned Miller to the Philippines a few weeks after the buzzing incident, he thanked God. "The war was in its final year, but as I look back, that transfer helped bring a ton of relief."

Despite his intentions to leave the military for good after his postwar discharge, Miller decided to make a career of it once he was called from the Marine reserves to active duty at the outbreak of the Korean War,

He went on to see combat in Korea and later served in the Vietnam War as well.

Was continuing to answer his country's call the former Henry County farm boy's way of making amends for helping to scare the wits out of his relatives and friends the day the mystery plane buzzed Paris?

One thing is certain, he didn't reveal his big secret until most of the folks who witnessed the daredevil feat had departed to their just rewards.

Carl Owens Juiced Up Old Time Molasses Making

C arl Owens didn't end the favorite old country way of making molasses, but he sure did revolutionize it. Owens — who grew up in the Elkhorn community of Henry County — carried on the molasses-making tradition borrowed from his ancestors. Just as his father did, he made molasses to sell to other farm families in the large cotton growing section of Southeast Henry County.

Owens brewed some of the best black strap molasses found in the South. Not only was the molasses delicious on hot buttered biscuits, but recommended by country doctors as a remedy for bad colds.

Owens' biggest problem in making "out of this world molasses," was that the doggone mule was too slow. As word spread into other counties about Owens' fine molasses, he began to be overwhelmed by orders.

"At the slow pace of making molasses with mule power, I couldn't begin to satisfy everybody," he said.

The advent of rural electrical power to the area in the latter 1940s, was the answer to Carl's problems. Although his neighbors reacted with skepticism, Owens came upon the idea he knew would be beneficial to other sorghum cane growers. Using a blueprint from the farmers friend, Sears Roebuck mail order catalog, the crafty Owens constructed a block building near his home. He vowed to replace the reliable mule with a gas powered operation.

Friends remained skeptical, wondering how Carl would combat the hot runoff steam. Owens' answer was a large exhaust fan in a window at one end of the building. He also built the interior of the house tight to reduce flies. Owens next installed a propane gas tank to divert gas to the cooker.

One good look, however, convinced Owens that the Sears engineers hadn't designed what he wanted.

Those engineers had just gone by the book ... they didn't know bull about a farmer in Henry County making sorghum molasses the way we folks like it.

"Listening to them cost me a lot of money, but I knew what I'd have to have in order to make 140 gallons of molasses a day. I also ended up having to install some 450 gallon stainless steel tanks."

Owens knew his work would have been in vain had his product been less in quality than the sorghum produced so long by his family. "To simply speed the process is of no worth if the true country taste is no longer in the product," he said,

His apprehension disappeared as that first batch — made without the old mule — came to the top and started to settle," he said,

"You never saw a prettier sight in your life," he recalled.

The economic effect was profound as well. Owens' gas-powered mill revolutionized his marketing process. Instead of taking a few gallons of sorghum to stores in Paris to sell, he began shipping orders to Michigan and other northern states.

"Once I took a load to Cadiz, Kentucky ... a grocer liked the sorghum so good he bought me out, even though he took a chance by violating the town's anti-peddling law.

"From then on I never had to go to Cadiz, the grocer came over to my farm to buy," asserted Owens.

Island No. 10 a Waterloo for Henry County Rebs

What do hundreds of Henry County natives have in common? Answer: Their ancestors were soldiers serving in the Confederate States of America's 46th Tennessee Infantry.

While true... that in itself wasn't so unique considering the times. When President Jefferson Davis pleaded for volunteers from the Confederate States, Henry County went all out to respond to the call.

However, with little time to train for battle, the CSA 46th was hastily ordered to Island Number 10 on the Mississippi River in Missouri. The Confederate high command hoped to thwart a Union invasion into Western Kentucky.

Unfortunately, the men sent from Henry County and other border counties were ill-equipped, many soldiers not even having a rifle.

According to family biographies submitted in the recently published Henry County History book, several dozen of their ancestors were taken prisoner at Island 10. They were placed in Union prison camps, mostly at Camp Douglas, Illinois.

However, most were paroled after taking an oath they would not take up arms against the North again. The vast majority of paroled Rebel soldiers broke their promise. Dozens rejoined their fellow Southerners and fought through the remainder of the war.

Among Paris Rebels captured was Benjamin Angel who enlisted for one year after he was recruited by Colonel Jonathon M. Clark on Nov.29, 1861. He was captured on April 8, 1862, and soon paroled at Camp Butler, Mo. It is not known whether Angel returned to the war.

One Henry County Rebel who avoided capture was Zachariah Byars. When Byars' regiment was overrun near Hickman, Ky., he eluded the Yankee patrols and swam across the backwaters of Reelfoot Lake to safety.

Also managing to escape a Union entrapment was William Harrison Key who returned to the Confederate cause and later fought behind General John Bell Hood in Middle Tennessee.

Probably the most famous of Henry County soldiers taken prisoner at Island No. 10 was Colonel Samuel Caldwell, M.D.. Caldwell was captured along with his first cousins Tom Dumas and Frank Dumas when their unit was surrounded by the enemy.

They and more than a dozen other captured Henry County soldiers were imprisoned at Camp Douglas before being paroled. Caldwell was freed before the others because the armies agreed to release captured medical officers.

However, Caldwell traveled to Port Hudson, La. where he contracted typhoid fever and almost died. He slowly regained his health and returned to Paris. There, he was recruited by General Nathan Bedford Forrest. He rode with Forrest and became the calvary leader's most trusted surgeon and saved the lives of wounded soldiers on both sides.

Had it not been for Caldwell, history might have changed drastically. The Northern press was outraged after reports that Forrest's men butchered both white and black Union soldiers at the Battle of Fort Pillow, which prompted investigations of Forrest.

Forrest was first called on the carpet by the Confederate government in Richmond and, after the war, was about to be tried by the United States for war crimes.

In both investigations, Caldwell testified that Forrest rode his horse between the Confede rates and Union defenders in an attempt to prevent the butchery,

Frank Dumas rejoined the efforts of his countrymen and died in the Battle of Atlanta in 1864.

When Marion Hastings was captured at Island Number 10, few in his regiment had guns to defend themselves. A local Civil War historian wrote after the war "that a few of Marion Hastings comrades in arms had an assortment of crude weapons such as squirrel rifles and old muskets."

After being paroled, Hastings was exchanged for Union prisoners in Vicksburg, Miss. He was promoted to second lieutenant and fought in the defense of Vicksburg.

Also exchanged at Vicksburg was Colonel Robert Armstrong Owens. Before that, he was shuttled around various Yankee prisons, going from Camp Douglas to Camp Chase, Ohio to Johnson Island in Lake Michigan.

Near Jackson, Miss., he was placed in command of both the 46th and 55th Tennessee regiments. Setting an example to his regiment — pinned down by Yankee sharpshooters — he exposed himself to feel out the enemy location.

A sharp-shooter concealed in plum thickets promptly shot a minnie ball through Owens' hand, disabling him for life.

John Dill Paschall, after he was captured at Island No. 10, was imprisoned at Johnson Island. Also exchanged at Vicksburg, Paschall was seriously wounded at Franklin Nov. 30, 1964, but still fought until the end of the war, including at the battle of Atlanta.

Obviously, the dogged determination by these and other former Confederate prisoners of the Tennessee 46th helped cement Henry County's immortality as the Volunteer County of the Volunteer State.

Wild Man - Creature
of McMinn County

Man, since Adam and Eve, has reacted with untold emotion when jilted by a woman he believed he was destined to marry. When that happened to Mason Kershaw Evans, he became mentally disjointed and left a good family and a promising career to find shelter in the wilds of Starr Mountain, where he lived for 40 years, surviving by eating snakes, grasshoppers and roots.

Evans was a brilliant teacher and a polished officer in the Tennessee militia. He was the envy of the settlers who lived along Conasauga Creek in rugged McMinn County, before the War for Southern Independence.

He was the principal of a two-teacher school in north McMinn County. Proud and self-disciplined, Mason rode a fine black steed to school early each morning. Unknown at the time, his life would peak and shatter because of the pretty young teacher hired to teach under him.

The son of a Quaker, since converted to an old time Baptist Holy Roller, Mason soon became attracted to the beautiful woman whose father was an elderly retired doctor and wealthy landowner. Mason and the woman began meeting rather casually — sometimes beneath the shade of a white oak — to discuss the progress of their pupils. Before long the tryst took on some romantic overtones and their talk turned to romance and wedded bliss.

On what fate would determine to be their final tryst, Evans asked the woman to marry him. They both seemed madly in love and neither thought too much of it when the lady said she would go home and tell her father. After all, it was once an unwritten rule in the South for lovers of good family stock to first receive the approval of the girl's daddy before marriage.

Had Evans known the type of stern aristocrat he craved for a future father-in-law he might have chosen to accompany his girl friend to her father's home and fall on his knees. The woman's father was a widowed man who watched over his daughter like a mother hen over chicks.

But when the young woman declared her love for Evans her father literally hit the ceiling. He knew about Evans' ambitions of become a career soldier.

The doctor angrily told his daughter that he would never stand for her marrying a military man who would be duty bound if ordered to spend months away from his wife and children to kill Indians.

To erase the hurt, the doctor finally relented from his bitterness at Evans and regained his daughter's confidence with promises of a dowry. He agreed to pay his daughter $1,000 immediately and deed to her his 350 acres of prime farm land.

Early the next morning, Evans was the epitome of worldly happiness. Saddling his horse, Mason galloped as fast as the mount could go to the little school house down on Conasauga Creek. At first he was not concerned that his girl hadn't arrived. But he was sure that the lady would be by his side by the time he rang the bell to summon the pupils.

When she still had not arrived, Evans combined the classes. He guessed that his true love was detained for some unexpected, but plausible reason.

However, as the day wore on and his sweetheart did not show, Mason was overcome with anxiety.

When finally it became time to dismiss the class, Evans had decided to saddle his faithful horse and ride like lightning to the doctor's farm.

However, as he started to mount, Evans saw the teacher step down from a buggy that was driven by one of her father's hired hands. Mason reached excitedly for his sweetheart's arms, expecting a warm embrace and pledge to join him beside the alter.

To Evans' utter surprise, she rebuffed his advances. NO! NO! NO! was her reaction. Nor would the lady provide any clue as to why Mason was suddenly a stranger in her life.

When the teacher coldly rebuffed Mason, he experienced the type of trauma, which he had known at fire and brimstone, primitive Baptist camp meetings along Conasauga Creek.

Turning away from the woman, Evans raced his horse to his parents home where he unsaddled and put the dependable mount in the barn. Without bothering to go in his mother's house for the usual supper, he headed up Starr Mountain. Dejected and tormented, Evans made his home in Panther Cave ... choosing to live the life of a hermit.

For the next 40 years, until his death, he would exist on wild berries, fruits, nuts and vegetables which he stole from farmers at the base of the mountain. He also learned to digest raw meat from rabbits, squirrels, and snakes.

His hair grew long over his shoulders, falling below the waist. His toenails and fingernails were long which caused him to look like some wild animal.

After a time, he picked up another human companion who, like Evans, had fled the responsibilities of life below and found refuge on Starr Mountain. At first, Mason felt challenged and often fought with the intruder.

Eventually, they became friends and huddled together in the cave to ward off bitter cold and snow. During warmer months, they covered themselves with leaves for protection and slept on the ground.

Mason become aware, not long after he settled in Panther Cave, that something earthshaking was happening.

He was startled one day by the sound of gunfire. At first Evans feared that angry farmers were attempting to harm him for his frequent evening raids on their gardens. But when he saw companies of gray clad soldiers carrying rifles, he felt that his country had been attacked by a foreign nation.

The sight brought more anxiety to Evans, who now feared that he could be arrested for being a deserter in time of war. Mason was unaware that his state and county had seceded from the United States. He had no way of knowing that his relatives and friends were now fighting to gain independence from the United States, he had so recently revered.

Evans also was watching when a large hotel called White Cliff was built below his hideout. Evans later ventured to the hotel and was fed quality food by friendly cooks. Later, the hotel employees would hang buckets of food from tree limbs for the wild man of the knobs.

Evans' quest to return to civilization was further fueled by workmen who were busy laying tracks for a new railroad from Athens to Tellico Plains. On moonlit nights, as he waited for friendly cooks to leave food outside the hotel kitchen, Mason was impressed by guests who discussed the Athens & Tellico Plains railroad. Once he heard the hotel manager express reservations about the railroad's future … whether it could prove profitable.

Nobody in McMinn County seemed concerned about Evans' longtime exile on Starr Mountain until a nosey Yankee journalist came to Athens and started a newspaper. The journalist learned about Evans' life as a hermit.

He resorted to write sensational stories about the Wild Man of the Mountains that often bordered on fiction. The Yankee editor also crusaded for Mason's capture by the authorities. It resulted in public outcry, and Mason was hunted down and brought to the McMinn County poor farm.

After a short time, Evans escaped to return to his home in the rugged mountains. Shortly afterward, his loyal brother-in-law J. Horner Coltharp — who had relatives living in Henry County — built Mason a hideout on his land so that the hermit could come and go, unmolested.

As in the case of the infamous outlaw Jessie James, the Northern press succeeded in building Evans up as a mountain character in the uncivilized mountains of East Tennessee. Ruthless Yankee journalists were bent on making Mason Evans a hillbilly celebrity who could sell a lot of books up North.

Their selfish dreams ended suddenly with the discovery of Mason's frozen still body on a mountainside, January 11, 1892. Coltharp claimed the remains. The tormented body of the Wild Man of Starr Mountain was placed in a crude wooden casket and buried in Hickory Grove Cemetery near his parents, who both had died of dreaded diptheria.

(From R. Frank McKinney's *Torment in the Knobs*)

Last of the Newspapers' Red Hot Mamas - Dan Hicks

If I leave this world knowing that I had lived to tell about just one of the following three challenges, I know my life in the next world will be richly rewarded. That is (1) landing on the moon (2) winning a barroom brawl in Moscow (3) working for Dan Hicks.

Obviously, I didn't come close to the first couple of challenges.

I did have the satisfaction of surviving two tours with Dan Hicks, unquestionably the last of the fire and brimstone weekly newspaper editors for which the rural South was once so famous for.

Hicks was the red hot mama for the *Democrat Observer* in Madisonville for more than a quarter of a century. He was a lot of things to a lot of people. For the little nobody in rural Monroe County, he was the man that hung the moon.

To the free-loading politician, he was a maverick who stood in the way of the bosses who ruled the roost. To the corrupt bootlegger and two-bit gambler who ran the road houses from Sweetwater to Tellico Plains, he was an S.O.B. who needed to be taught the uncivil side of the law.

To the big shot businessmen who wanted no fame for their occasional tryst in dimly lit taverns and houses of ill repute, Hicks was the upstart editor who couldn't be bought. Even his colleagues who owned other newspapers in the East Tennessee mountains disliked the man. To many of them he was an uncompromising fool who couldn't write two sides of a story if it killed him. Most politicians despised and distrusted Hicks with a passion. Though a Democrat by family tradition, he would just as quickly burn a Democrat caught for a petty offense, as he would print the name of the Republican legislator caught for DWI.

More often than not, his one-man crusading against corruption in Monroe County — as well as other counties in southeast Tennessee — often got him in trouble. How and why it didn't get him killed at least dozens of times, is likely known only by the great man upstairs.

Because of his war on bootleggers and cutthroat gamblers, he was beaten and left for dead in the dark alleys of Madisonville. His newspapers were burned at least once. He probably received as many threats on his life as Confederate raider Nathan Bedford Forrest did from the Yankee command in Washington, D.C. during the War for Southern Independence.

Even the supposedly lawful arm of the law made it rough on the messenger with a message. Frustrated once because bootleggers were seemingly given a free hand to practice their illegal trade, Hicks decided to at least have some fun with the Madisonville law.

He wrote strong editorials about bootleggers selling beer at all hours of the night, pointing out that most had been convicted of felonies and unable to hold a legal license.

He also announced that if the felons could get by with selling beer and bonded whiskey, he thought he ought to be able to do likewise. A public notice in the *Democrat* gave the day and exact hour when Hicks would sell beer in front of his newspaper, and to heck with a license.

Hicks really didn't need to be so accommodating to city hall ... they were long ready for an excuse to bust the annoying editor. The minute one of Madisonville's town drunks passed money to Hicks for a six pack of beer, the law pounced. He was handcuffed and locked in jail.

If the city judge merely meant to scare Hicks and watch him come begging for freedom, that judge must still be searching for traction.

After an hour or so, Hicks was told he could go. Then after the fiery editor stayed put, he was told to go. "Hell no ... I'm no better than the rest of the crooks," mocked Dan.

Unknown to the police, Hicks had rehearsed his act beforehand. While he was doing his time in the Madisonville lockup, his trusted staff back at the *Democrat* was calling every television station and big city daily in the country. It was a scoop about that small town editor who was being persecuted by the Madisonville police for doing his job.

Hicks wasn't about to make bond and leave jail, despite the pleadings of the law. At least not until he'd made a freight train load of hay out of his confinement. Before Hicks finally agreed to make bond, virtually every television network and news outlet across the United States knew about this crusading editor in the East Tennessee mountains who dared stand his ground against small town injustice.

Hicks was his own investigative reporter, often coming up with scoops about wrong doing with tips coming from suspect sources.

Although operating newspapers that published no more than twice a week, he often broke sensational stories about rampant and violent crime in Monroe, McMinn or Loudon counties. More than once, red-faced editors for large dailies in Chattanooga and Knoxville followed through on Dan's scoops. At times it came after their own articles were delayed for fear of libel suits.

It was Hicks — the dauntless country editor — who broke one of the most violent serial crimes to ever happen in the Tellico mountains.

For months, Joe Shepherd — a hard drinking, fast living resident of the Tellico Plains area — had been the leading suspect in the disappearance of two young teenage girls. In fact Shepherd had been with one of the victims within the last few minutes she was seen alive.

Like a pit bull on a bear hunt, Hicks relentlessly pursued the mystery for months. Through bitterly cold winters, he waded waist deep snow on the Tellico Mountains where Shepherd had knowingly walked with the girl on her last day of life.

Hicks persisted, even after other newspapers had determined to let nature take its course. Nature did take its course, when on a spring day, the thawing ground unleashed the haunting arm of a 16-year old female right through the top of what had been her hastily dug grave.

Hicks was believed to have been the first on the scene, after the grisly discovery was made by a woman who lived in the house near the girl's grave. The evidence pointed even more to Shepherd, who lived in that vicinity.

Obviously years ahead of his time, Hicks shocked most everyone, including the Knoxville newspapers, by publishing the picture of the pitiful girl's out-stretched arm on the front page of his newspaper.

Hicks may also have been behind his times ... at least the times when small town crusading editors were nearly a dime a dozen. In a day when mollycoddling newspaper publishers have caved in for fear of losing the mighty advertising dollar, Hicks continued to write it as he saw it.

If the pampered son of his biggest advertiser was arrested for driving while intoxicated, Hicks refused to cover-up. To him, if the lowest town drunk's name was to appear on the police blotter ... why not the big shot's spoiled brat.

Indeed, such honest reporting did finally damage Hicks financially. The big moneyed people — some because of politics — pulled their ads and gave them to *The Advocate*, his competitor in Sweetwater.

It was only a matter of time before the competitor — owned by a Greeneville-based chain — bit heavily into Hick's pocketbook. The last of the red hot mamas had fallen to the paper with the least spine.

Hicks' paper still had the most readership ... the little people. Unfortunately, the little fellows' bankroll was far less than the hefty billfolds of the rich and powerful.

Hicks put the paper — which had been in his family for generations — up for sale. He hoped against hope that he wouldn't have to sell the *Democrat* to his opposition which was now a monopoly throughout East Tennessee.

When he couldn't find a suitable buyer, Hicks sold to the John Jones family who obviously knew all along that the red hot mama would finally offend one big advertiser one time too many. Respecting Hicks newspaper savvy and popularity as a tell-it-like-it-is crusader, the new owners extracted a written clause from Hicks that he would not start a competing newspaper within a 35-mile radius for five years.

Over the years since leaving Madisonville, I have returned often to reunite with a score of friends. The one thing I hear most is how people miss the journalistic bravery of Dan Hicks and their public scorn for the mealy-mouthed *Advocate*.

Five years are up and my friends in Monroe County say that Hicks hasn't started a new paper. But then, what can we really expect from a gutsy editor who has survived arson, bullets and even dreaded cancer.

A brave editor? Whatever more could one say about him. How many other journalists do you know who have won the National Quill Award for Courageous news reporting?

The Buford Pusser of
East Tennessee

They called him the Buford Pusser of the East Tennessee hills. But to his loyal supporters in the mountains of Sevier County, the fighting barber — Millard "Bat" Gibson — was the bravest crime-buster who wore a badge.

Gibson, a hearty mountaineer who grew up in the Tenth District of Sevier County, was a barber with a gift for talk that made sense. He had as many customers as a passenger train could haul.

Around election time, his barbershop became a political hangout ... suddenly the weather wasn't important.

One day, Bat decided he'd run for constable and was easily elected. In Tennessee, the office of constable has long been regarded as a joke, and maybe that's unfair.

Anyway, Bat Gibson took the job seriously and sometimes his zeal for arresting lawbreakers before the sheriff or chief of police could, drew their ire.

When the county fair came to Sevierville in the mid 1960s, Gibson made war on the carnival rip-offs, especially the sharks who did the old cup and peas trick.

A mountaineer named Ogle, whom everybody liked, complained to a highway patrolman that he was cheated out of his pay check by one of the con men.

The highway patrolman told Ogle he first needed proof, and anyway, the rip-off artist — who happened to be a big chested woman — claimed Ogle was "just talking."

Bat who was affectionately dubbed the "Batman" during his law enforcing years, heard the conversation, and to the chagrin of the trooper, "butted in."

The trooper told Gibson that he had investigated and found nothing wrong. Bat told the trooper that the fair was in his district and more or less reminded the officer about his duty on the highways.

"Who was the woman that stole you blind, old timer?" he asked Ogle. Ogle pointed out the woman who operated one of the trick gambling tables.

Gibson noticed that the man had berry stain on his hands and knew Ogle had just returned from blackberry picking.

Bat approached the woman and demanded she "return $300 you stole from one of our citizens."

The woman smirked, but the ever alert Gibson saw a wad of cash in the big woman's bra. Gibson grabbed the wad of bills and saw they had berry stains.

"That your money old timer?"

By morning, the word that Gibson had recovered Ogle's money mushroomed through the hills. It was certain that Bat would be the next high sheriff. After all, what greater deed can a lawman do than to stand up for the common folks.

Gibson was unbeatable during his three two-year terms. However, Tennessee law at the time forbade a sheriff from seeking a fourth consecutive term.

Bat was afraid of no man who walked, and there were some awful mean people in the hollers of Sevier County. Gibson meant to enforce the law and did, if that meant cracking the head of some drunk resister ... so be it.

Gibson decided to take on some of the high and mighty in Gatlinburg who more or less laughed at "this hick of a sheriff from the lower end."

Gatlinburg was totally dry and Gibson was determined that hotels would not have alcohol on the premises. The state Jaycees were having their convention at one of the hotels the following weekend. Jaycees, of course, are notorious party people, and brought plenty of cases of whiskey.

Gibson had given them advanced warning. "There would be no drinking in his county." Gatlinburg's big shots continued to smirk and all but dared the sheriff to raid in their town.

The Jaycees were drinking it up and wondering about that hick sheriff.

They soon learned, when doors were flung open and there was Bat with a small army of overall clad deputies. The "overhaul gang" with their star badges, was indeed an eye openers for the Jaycees.

Gibson carried out his threat, and in so doing, angered Gatlinburg city council and hotel operators, who vowed to beat him in the next election.

The 'haves' were not a fraction as plentiful as the 'have nots.' Gibson was reelected and warned Gatlinburg's leaders that he wouldn't let up as long as the law was being broken.

The city's answer was to vote in beer, but whiskey sales remained illegal. Bat heard that whiskey was being bootlegged big time on Mount Harrison where Gatlinburg Ski Lodge was located.

Once again, Bat and the overhauls struck, blitzing into the ballroom to see patrons pouring blended whiskey down.

Gibson looked over the bar and saw several cabinets that were padlocked. He asked the bartender to unlock the cabinets. The barkeep claimed that he didn't have keys in his possession.

"Go get my crowbar, Pink," he ordered loyal deputy, Pink Rhyhuff.

By the time Pink returned, the barkeep had remembered he had the keys after all. As the cabinets were unlocked, Bat and his men began stacking pints and fifths of whiskey and vodka in boxes.

Gibson may not have attended a single police academy, but what he lacked in formality, he made up for in pure courage and common sense. There was a good amount of daring involved, too. Once he chased three suspected car thieves into Knox County, exchanging shots with the outlaws as the cars sped down Chapman Highway.

The crooks were eventually caught at a roadblock, manned by Knox county deputies and the highway patrol, but the fighting barber took the men back to Knox County.

When Gibson returned to the Sevier County jail, one of his deputies noticed a trace of blood on the side of his head. "You've been hit, sheriff," said a worried deputy.

Sure enough, Gibson had been creased by one of the flying bullets aimed his way.

Controversy was never a stranger to Gibson. Angered when he saw a black man from Knoxville with a white girl in the seat beside him, he stopped the car in Pigeon Forge.

The colored man made the mistake of sassing the sheriff. Gibson beat the man senseless, causing him to be permanently paralyzed.

Incidents such as that were drawing reaction from a Knox County magistrate and *News-Sentinel* columnist.

For weeks, the writer, Willard Yarbrough, hounded Gibson in his columns. One night, Yarbrough made the mistake of drinking at a Gatlinburg bar. Gibson's overhaul gang pulled him over near Sevierville and Yarbrough was charged with drunk driving.

Bat didn't put Yarbrough in the tank with the rest of the drunks. Instead he put Yarbrough in a tiny cell beside the coal furnace.

The furnace grew hotter and hotter, and by the time Yarbrough was bailed out by friends, he had nearly dehydrated.

Bat was never elected again, although he always ran close. By then the population in Gatlinburg had exploded with new residents, and the established made sure they didn't vote for the Batman ... the Buford Pusser of East Tennessee.

A Few Yellowdogs

T here ought to be some kind of law against people who would sooner make bread with their worst enemy, over their best friend — if it turned out that their worst enemy was a Democrat and the best friend a Republican. But that can happen in some parts of Tennessee — certainly in the counties of Henry, Monroe, and Weakley.

You take Howard Smith of Dresden, for instance. When Howard really likes you, there's no better friend. Howard will walk down the road with you on the gloomiest of mornings and buy you a beer at the American Legion club.

He'll fish beside you for catfish in the Obion River until the cows come home and be the first to come visit, should you wind up in the hospital. There's only one thing that could get in the way of such airtight friendship ... even though it may be only of short duration.

I've learned that the best time to be far away from Howard is in the weeks before a presidential, gubernatorial, or most any election where partisan politics are involved, especially if you call yourself a Republican.

Howard is one of those fiery yellowdog Democrats, and around Howard — when there's a partisan election — don't mention facts, even if you know you're right. When there's Republican against Democrat, Howard just won't let facts get in his way, and that's what you mean when you call someone a genuine, yellowdog Democrat.

In 1990 when I lived in Madisonville, I was the Republican nominee for state public service commissioner for the East Tennessee grand division.

During Christmas vacation, I came over to Northwest Tennessee to visit my mother in Paris and other relatives in my native Henry County.

I also made it a point to cross the Weakley County line to visit old friends at the Dresden Elks Lodge. First drinking buddy I ran across was Howard Smith.

"Spider, old buddy ... I want to buy you a beer," were Howard's first words, following a stout handshake. The next words Howard spoke might have sounded rude to a Yankee stranger, but to me were typical, from a redneck who is your true friend 99 percent of the time.

"I didn't vote for you in the election," he eyeballed me in the most candid manner.

I said … "old buddy, thanks for the beer, even if you did vote for my opponent. But the election's over, let's drink a toast to our friendship and the real spirit of Christmas."

Howard raised his glass to the ceiling as he bought another round.

"No offense — you and I have been friends a long time — but I was raised a Democrat. My grandpappy and pappy were Democrats and they'd have turned over in their graves if I had voted for you," added Smith.

I kind of played devil's advocate by, saying. "Howard, old friend, has my opponent ever bought you a drink and walked down the road with you, like I have many times?"

"Certainly not … I don't even like the man, but he knows better than to be a Republican, and you don't," said Howard.

Take the case of my cousin Buddy Callicott who married my cousin, Martha Ross. We were all raised around Osage and Cottage Grove, before winding up in Paris. We are still country folks at heart … the only thing that's changed is that I turned Republican and they're still Democrats, like their pappys and grandpappys.

Buddy, for sure, is what you call a yellowdog Democrat. Buddy will tell you right now, that he'd sooner vote for the devil so long as that devil was the only Democrat on the ticket. That's what you call a yellowdog Democrat all right.

For several years, Buddy and Martha lived in Athens up in southeast Tennessee, because that's where his job took him. Understand they liked Athens and McMinn County real fine. What Buddy didn't like was being in Republican country. He couldn't wait to get back to Henry County where there's so few Republicans, they hold their mass conventions in telephone booths.

My brother likes to needle Buddy about his yellowdog Democrat politics, although they are the very best of friends. A few years ago, Buddy and Martha decided to take a vacation out west and borrowed a truck camper from Bill Dumas.

Bill stuck a Bush sticker on a part of the camper where he figured old Buddy wouldn't see it, but most everybody else would. The story is that Buddy didn't see the Bush sticker until after he and Martha started home.

Don't you know that Buddy did a lot of bragging in places like Texas, New Mexico and Wyoming about Clinton beating Bush for president. And I wonder if folks — noticing that Bush sticker — aren't thinking ... darn, that Tennessee must have a lot of mugwamps.

George Bellamy in Sweetwater was a good friend of mine. I was sorry to hear about George's passing after I left Monroe County and moved back to Paris.

George was a true yellowdog Democrat, but he wasn't exactly like most yellowdogs.

George would argue with you over politics until the cows came home. But he'd never raise his voice, get mad or lose that familiar s..t-eating grin. George would listen to you and tell you, matter of fact, that he respected your right to be a Republican. But in his heart, George knew he was right and somewhere during a course of conversation, he'd say that "my daddy was a Democrat and when they put that last spade of dirt over me, the world know's there went another good Democrat."

George asked me to go by the big cemetery in Sweetwater once.

Said he wanted me to see his father's grave. George being a friend I could always count on, I was only too glad to comply with his wishes.

When we reached the Bellamy plot, he suddenly pointed very proudly to his father's tombstone. The epitaph at the top read. "He was a good Democrat." Beyond the slightest doubt, it still runs in the family.

J.D. Styles was born high on a ridge in Cocke County, where they still have to plant corn with a mule. J.D. lived most of his adult life in Sevier County, just outside of Pigeon Forge.

J.D. came to be known as one of the county's best carpenters and built a lot of homes. J.D. was different than most builders in that he was a proud yellowdog Democrat who didn't try to hide it.

Most builders wouldn't tell you their politics — much less discuss it with a ten foot pole.

Styles was different though. He'd bad-mouth Richard Nixon or Ronald Reagan just when he was writing an ardent Republican his total bill.

There was a day, back in the late years of the Great Depression when J.D. would have starved to death if he opened his mouth about being a Democrat.

Sevier County was such a Republican bastion that when one of the few Democrats died, they wouldn't let him be buried in the graveyard with Republicans. They'd bury him out in some hay field by himself.

That began to change when prosperity hit Gatlinburg and Pigeon Forge, and with it, the second invasion of damn Yankees.

That wouldn't have changed J.D., though. He'd rather starve to death planting corn on Cocke County rocky ridges than desert his Democrat raising for big Republican bucks.

In the 1970s there still weren't a lot of folks in Sevier County admitting to be Democrats. But at least they had left the telephone booth.

Nevertheless, there was a serious rift between what few Democrats lived in Sevierville and what few Democrats lived in Gatlinburg. The Democrats in Sevierville wanted to overthrow the county chairman, Walter Hall, who was a Gatlinburg yellowdog.

Paul Henderson, the yellowdog Democrat kingpin who lived just outside Sevierville, asked Styles to run against Hall.

The Sevierville Democrats knew that Styles wasn't a public speaker or polished in procedure. But they knew J.D. was as honest as the day was long and thought that Styles was the only Democrat who could beat Hall.

Styles did beat Hall, and pretty good too. One thing Gatlinburg folks — whether they are Democrats or Republicans — have in common, is that they don't like to lose to Sevierville.

When the next election for chairman came up, the Gatlinburg folks were ready for blood and primed for revenge. The Sevierville Democrats were equally prepared to defend their title in this "second War of the Roses."

Styles was renominated, while Gatlinburg picked Bruce Reagan.

Well, when it came time for the fierce election, so many people showed up that even the courtroom wasn't big enough to seat them.

Of course, most of them — at least 75 percent — were Republicans. Such a thing can happen in Tennessee, which has no party voter registration law.

They moved the election to a maintenance garage owned by the county, but at least one-half of the estimated 400 people were forced to stand.

Normally, when there is a contested election at Democrat mass conventions, stand-up votes are called. It seemed that the leaders of the two factions had been similarly successful at rounding up Republican support. About one-half of the voters seated stood up for Reagan and the other one-half stood up for Styles.

That made it impossible to accurately count the dozens who were standing at the rear. Not wishing to break tradition by, of all things, calling for a 'sit-down' vote, attorney Ben Brabson Jr. — the chief election officer — threw up his hands and called for another election the following Saturday.

Old-fashioned Southern electioneering lasted around the clock and many half pints of whiskey were brought from Gatlinburg to bribe voters in Frog Alley, a low income Sevierville neighborhood. Brabson also announced the next election would have to be done by secret ballot. This sharp break from tradition saddened old line Democrats who had pride in letting the world see their true colors.

There was a big snow on the ground the next Saturday, so the election was postponed for a week. There was a big snow on the ground the following Saturday, but the people came in droves. It seemed the crowd was even bigger. A look about ascertained that both sides had recruited new Republican faces, along with the old.

In what undoubtedly was the largest turnout for a county party election in many years, the election consumed several hours.

The counting took at least an hour, before Brabson nervously announced that Styles had the most votes. The Gatlinburg crowd hollered foul, claiming the election had been stolen. There were charges from both sides that people had been seen voting two or three times or more.

The moral of the donnybrook is that while no Democrat has ever been elected in a partisan election in Sevier County, the yellowdogs clearly claimed the limelight in the long winter vote.

The Notorious White Caps

I *do solemnly swear before God and Man that if I reveal anything concerning our organization or anything we may do, the penalty shall be to receive — 100 lashes — and to leave the country within ten days or to be put to death. Now I take this oath freely and voluntarily and am willing to abide by the obligation in every respect. I further agree and swear before God that if I reveal anything concerning our organization, I will suffer my throat to be cut; my heart to be shot out and my body to be burned. That I will forfeit my life, my property and all that I have in the world to come — so help me God.*

• • •

A few years after I moved to Sevier County I was seated in a popular restaurant drinking coffee and chewing the fat with my mountain friends at what rebel flag raising Southerners fondly call the liars table.

You've heard the expression ... it gets so deep around the liars table, you had better wear knee high boots. It was no exception at Johnson's Drive-In where folks like Sam Hodges, Harry Patty and Phil Wynn — all steeped deeply in Sevier County roots — idled the time away with homespun jargon.

Then it befell on me — my steeped Tennessee roots are in West Tennessee — to throw a monkey wrench into this cordial morning with a careless slip of the tongue. Since moving to the area — particularly after landing a job as reporter at the local newspaper, I had been fascinated with the history about the Sevier County White Caps.

The day before, I had been walking through historic Shiloh Cemetery nearby and came upon the grave of Pleas Wynn. Wynn had the infamous distinction of being one of the last two people to die by legal hanging in Sevier County.

Wynn went to the gallows in Sevierville along with Catlett Tipton in 1901. Their crime was membership in the dreaded White Caps ... charged with two of the dozens of brutal murders committed by the lawless White Caps during an eight-year reign of terror.

My crime was in blurting out that I finally discovered the grave of the last man hung in Sevier County.

I realized that I had a bad case of foot in the mouth disease when my close pal, J. Roy Miller, started literally kicking my shins off. Sevier County — despite losing much originally because of galloping tourism and the second invasion of Yankees — continues to hold on to its close-knit, clannish ways.

The biggest mistake a stranger can make, especially a transplant from up North, is to talk derogatorily about natives in the East Tennessee mountains. The odds are great that a relative will be in hearing distance. In such instances, diarrhea of the mouth can be harmful to one's health.

On that day — when the last thing I wanted was to lose the respect and friendship of people who are hard enough to win over — I should have had the sense to know that Phil Wynn, a prominent Sevierville attorney, had the same surname as the long dead White Cap.

Phil Wynn was the great nephew of Pleas Wynn, and the late White Cap had himself been a member of a just as prominent family of Phil's ancestors who lived in the last century.

It's a fact that many of the White Caps were among the cream of the crop … doctors, lawyers, merchants, and educators.

So were many of their descendants, and that is why the bloody White Caps have remained one of the county's best kept secrets.

Call it fear of reprisal, social standing, or ignorance. But even respected historians and newspaper editors have succeeded in covering up this dark history, as though fearing the oath itself.

Once, I had a call from a Sevierville native whose grandfather had been one of the principal lawmen prosecuting Wynn and Tipton. He had a very rare picture which he thought the newspaper might want to publish in a special Sevier County bicentennial edition.

It was a photograph of Sevier County Deputy Sheriff Tom Davis escorting two fugitive White Caps from the train depot.

The owner of the newspaper was Bill Postlewaite, a kind and generous native of Miami, Ohio. Postlewaite was the complete opposite of the hard-boiled, chain-smoking editor who yells at cub reporters and thrives on sensationalism to sell papers.

The fine gentleman was so sensitive about the natives in his adopted home he refused to even allow mention about the White Caps in his newspaper. Woe be the reporter or editor who disagreed.

But Bill and I — despite our stout loyalty to our different sections of the nation ... divided by the War for Southern Independence — were as close as any rebel and Yankee could be.

When I told Bill about the potential of the picture as a feature for the paper's bicentennial special, he agreed — breaking a long-standing rule never to print anything about the White Caps.

However, to find out the identities of the two White Caps photographed I called Beulah Lynn, the Sevier County historian, and a gracious lady.

The lady was aghast that I could even think of reviving the White Caps in the newspaper. She went so far as reminding me that Bob Catlett, the White Cap leader, was an ancestor of many prominent modern day Catletts, including the society editor for our newspaper. She also pointed out that a well known county legislator and bank president was also a descendant of White Caps.

She was also convinced I had no intention of backing down from using a photograph that had so much potential. About midnight, though, I responded to my ringing telephone at home. It was my boss, Postlewaite. Ever so apologetic, Bill told me that he had been called by "certain" important citizens in Sevierville who did not want the photograph published ... not even for the special bicentennial section.

I was crushed, but I also was filled with respect for Bill Postlewaite. I couldn't hide my disappointment when I returned the photograph back to the owner. Yet, I was convinced that the descendant of Sheriff Tom Davis expected as much.

The organization started in the mountain community of Pittman Center with Puritan intentions that captivated the good moral Christians. In the early 1890s, the God-fearing Christians were concerned because prostitutes and lewd characters were moving from Knoxville and corrupting their peaceful communities. Most of the misfits congregated in Copeland Creek, east of Gatlinburg. Copeland Creek, now a ghost community inside the Smoky Mountain National Park, was already regarded as a dangerous place to practice decency because it was a haven for moonshiners and other rough people.

Some of the area's decent citizens decided that it was God's will that the immoral ilk be driven away. That was the origin of the White Cap organization, also referred to as "white capping."

The lewd individuals, as well as residents suspected of adultery or mistreating their families, were notified to leave the area or receive a severe whipping on their bare backs with hickory sticks or thorny vines.

Hickory wreaths were nailed on the doors of suspected evil people as a grim warning. Obviously, the prostitutes and other lewd characters were initially unimpressed with the warnings, feeling secure in their backsliding environment. Then the White Caps made good on their threats.

Some eight to ten prostitutes were taken captive in Emerts Cove by heavily armed men wearing white hoods and white robes. They were severely whipped and ordered to leave the community immediately or face worse punishment.

The women didn't have to be warned a second time, but hurried back to Knoxville to practice their illicit trade. Needless to say, the Emert's Cove incident was well received and brought White Caps their greatest moment of respect from decent people.

The White Caps grew rapidly into what might be called a city state headed by a military dictatorship. It was able to do so largely because its early leaders were powerful citizens ... some the most wealthy of landowners. The organization was so strong, secretive, and set in fraternal law, that no White Cap had fear of being convicted in a court of law.

There were no juries selected that did not include White Caps. When a fellow White Cap was tried, it was pointed out by prearranged signals so that White Caps on the jury would know the defendant was a member. For years, White Caps were acquitted or freed by hung juries, regardless of their crimes.

It is doubtful that any of the original books written about the lawless organization remain, unless they are stored in the attics of long deceased White Caps. Those first books — it is said — spared no gory or blood-filled details and of course came direct from the horse's mouth.

Over the years, original books were rounded up by former leaders like Catlett or other prominent people involved in white capping and destroyed.

The fact that law abiding citizens like the county historian wanted to erase the memory of the dreaded White Caps further interfered with an accurate historical recording of what undoubtedly is the most infamous period in Tennessee history.

A prime reason is that writers with the talent to record the infamous deeds of the White Caps feared retaliation. After all, the organization did not die with the hanging of Wynn and Tipton. Many of the feared and more powerful leaders were still alive and even regarded as the cream of the crop, including Bob Catlett.

Fortunately, there were a few people of courage who did not want the White Cap movement to be erased from the face of the earth. Included was Mariam Mangrum, the county's first female legislator, and the incomparable Knoxville politician and grocer, Cas Walker.

Walker, who was born in rural east Sevier County, knew the hard life of a coal miner before settling in Knoxville and eventually founding a chain of successful cut-rate super markets. Walker, who resorted to unorthodox gimmicks like throwing live chickens from roofs of his stores to crowds below, became an idol of the masses of Knoxville's poor and working class.

He ran for a city council seat and his populist rapport with both black and white blue collar people made him an unbeatable political force for decades.

Walker was the ideal person to revise and bring back the dark era of Sevier County white capping. His father, Tom Walker, had been a forceful member of the Sevier County Blue Bills, a vigilante movement organized to oppose white capping.

The organization was formed out of desperation because local law enforcement was at an extreme disadvantage. There also was no likelihood of the state or federal government interfering in local matters.

The leader of the Blue Bills was Dr. Z.D. Massey of Sevierville, who finally resorted to an eye for an eye attitude, after treated patients who were badly beaten and left near death by the raiding White Caps. The Blue Bill strategy was to send spies among the ranks of White Caps to learn if the lawless group had plans to attack citizens. They, like the calvary in the War for Southern Independence, would ride their horses hell bent to leather to intercept their enemy.

The most famous of all White Cap-Blue Bill confrontations occurred on a chilled November night in 1894 near Pigeon Forge. Like armies, the opposing sides met on a wooded hill near the Little Pigeon River. Residents were startled to hear hundreds of shots exchanged. At least eight riders were killed or wounded.

The historic site became known as Battle Hill and had it not been for the determination of the county's leaders to blot out all mention of white capping, monuments and historic markers might have directed visitors to the spot. As it was, the boom of tourism and quest for Yankee dollars brought residential development.

Pleas Wynn and Catlett Tipton

*The hanging of these two men in the courthouse yard at
Sevierville brought the terror of the White Caps and
Blue Bills of Sevier County to an end, even though the
hatred fomented by this hooded gang yet lives on in
Sevier County and in the surrounding counties where
the kin of the White Caps and Blue Bills still live.*

One brutal incident that probably led to the formation of the Blue Bills was the ambush of respected Wears Valley farmer, Aaron McMahan, in July 1896. Ironically, he was shot dead by two of his own nephews, Newt Green and Wes Hendricks.

The bloody incident — resembling the infamous feuds between the McCoys of West Virginia and Hatfields of Kentucky — started weeks before. McMahan's daughter had married James Clabough, a poor but well-liked laborer.

Clabough's wife was accused by the White Caps of cheating on her husband. Bent on teaching her a lesson, several White Caps, including Green and Hendricks, broke into the Clabough home. Mrs. Clabough was abducted and given a severe whipping.

McMahan, who was incensed, swore out warrants on his nephews and others. The day after, the White Caps were given a hearing before a Wears Valley justice of the peace. McMahan, his son and son-in-law, were returning from a mill at Pigeon Forge with a wagon load of wheat. (That mill, which was built in 1836 and is owned now by Bob and Kathy Simmons, is one of the state's most popular tourist attractions.)

While passing through Little Cove in their wagon team, the family was ambushed. McMahan was mortally wounded and later died, although Dr. Massey did all in his power to save him. Clabough was shot through the neck and the younger McMahan received a lesser wound. Both later recovered.

The McMahan murder was one of many White Cap raids in which dozens of innocent people were killed or beaten. Thanks to the courage of Mrs. Mangrum and Walker, enough first hand accounts were written to immortalize this shameful part of history. Brief accounts of other terrible acts of white capping, which the author gained from both sides, will be given.

The fallacy, which perhaps separates this history from other examples of night riding lawlessness, is that no woman suspected of being unfaithful or of committing adultery was spared from a fate equal to death.

A shining example, which Walker described as unparalleled cruelty, was the whipping of Mary Breeden and two of her daughters. The family — which included a son , said to be a man of good character — awoke one night in early spring to find the house surrounded by numerous White Caps.

While some of the hooded men kept the son at bay with cocked guns, other night riders pulled Bell, the oldest daughter, from her bed. Taken outside under the moonlight, the helpless young woman was beaten to a bloody pulp by two men with leather whips.

Martha, her younger sister, was also lashed severely.

After Mrs. Breeden tried to intervene to help her daughters, the furious White Caps turned on the mother. Angered by the woman's interference, the White Caps gave the 60-year-old Mrs. Breeden an unmerciful beating which proved fatal. Mary might have saved her life, had she admitted White Cap accusations that her daughters were involved in adultery.

In the sultry summer of 1892, Eli Williamson was interrupted by two unwelcome visitors at his log house in Emerts Cove. One of the intruders, Bill Sneed, carried a rifle. Houston Romines, his companion, pulled a knife.

Williamson raised his arms and begged the men not to harm him. Sneed shot him in the chest. Williamson's fatal mistake was that he dared protect a woman whom the White Caps tried to whip a few nights before. Williamson and Henry Proffitt happened to be with Julia Ramsey when the White Caps kicked down her door. Her protectors opened fire, and Lewellan Sneed, brother of Bill Sneed, was slightly wounded. Eli Williamson died for defending a defenseless woman.

The downfall of white capping may have begun with the brutal murder of respected Sevierville physician, Dr. J.H. Henderson. Sitting by his fire place one night, Henderson's head was blown off by an assassin hidden outside his window.

The White Caps had plotted to abduct Henderson several weeks before, but Henderson was alerted by a Blue Bill who had infiltrated White Cap ranks.

Bill Guess was arrested and charged with the murder of Henderson, but was acquitted, showing that White Caps still had the ability to pack juries.

One of the last acts of terror by White Caps more directly involved the leader, Bob Catlett. Catlett, a wealthy landowner in the lower end of the county between Seviervillle and Seymour, was attempting to force a tenant, Walter Maples, to leave a house owned by Catlett without delay.

He had promised the house to William and Laura Whaley who would live there as share croppers.

When Maples refused Catlett's orders to leave immediately, Catlett rendered the deadly White Cap oath to Mrs. Whaley. He forced her at gun point to write a threatening note to Maples, warning him in typical white capping fashion to leave or face death.

Catlett then made the Whaleys don masks and accompany him to the shack where Maples lived. After the Whaleys tossed stones against the house and Catlett fired buckshot inside, Maples got the message and finally left.

Months later, Catlett threatened to have William Whaley arrested, accusing the share cropper of selling corn that belonged to Catlett. The worry and anxiety may have led to Laura's giving birth to a premature baby. After the baby was born, Rou Catlett, a respected school teacher and Bob Catlett's daughter, stopped by to congratulate the new mother.

During the course of the visit, Laura blurted out that Rou's father had forced her to take the White Cap oath and to help carry out a White Cap act of terror.

That evening, Rou, who was as decent as her father was evil, confronted her father in a rebellious tone. She probably didn't know that her own father was so incensed that Laura had violated the oath that he was bent on deadly revenge.

Catlett confronted William and Laura the next morning, warning that those who violated the oath were marked for certain death. The Whaleys and their infant daughter quickly moved to a nearby log cabin owned by Captain E. M. Wynn, the respected father of white capper Pleas Wynn.

In the meantime, word of Laura's confession to Rou Catlettt had leaked to Sheriff Davis. The high sheriff summoned Laura to the July 1896 term of grand jury. The courageous woman told the truth, although she knew it would cost her life.

On Dec. 28, 1896, Laura knew that Bob Catlett had kept his word. Two men suddenly burst into the Whaley's door. They were Pleas Wynn and Catlett Tipton, who were high on bootleg whiskey bought in Pigeon Forge.

Also in the cabin was Lizzie Chandler, Laura's sister. Knowing that she was about to die a violent death for violating the sacred oath, she handed her baby to Lizzie, who was lying in bed. Then she was executed along with her husband. Uncharacteristically, the White Caps had left a competent witness, Lizzie Chandler.

Town Drunk Ended Sunday
Beer Sales in Paris

Paris, Tennessee, has had some notable citizens in its 173-year history. Among them ... Governor James D. Porter, Civil War Governor Isham G. Harris and John Wesley Crockett. But none has quite become a household name in every walk of life as much as a rather crude character who grew up in the years before the Great Depression.

Wes Wisehart wasn't a saint by any means, but it would be unkind to call the man a hopeless sinner. Not that Wes didn't have his share of rowdy ways. That's what made him a local legend ... discussed to this day in low places as well as church aisles.

Wisehart, whose legacy includes a few terms as constable, is remembered as a rounder, known for his frequent bouts with whiskey and other spirits seven days a week.

Old timers will tell you that — despite Wisehart's hard drinking — his greatest legacy was bringing a halt to once legal Sunday beer sales in Paris.

The late Jack Brockwell, who operated money-making pool rooms in Paris throughout his adult life, often told customers about the day that Wes personally brought a ban on legal Sunday sale of beer or any alcoholic beverage in the Henry County seat.

Brockwell also had firsthand information on his side. He and his brother, Dick Brockwell, were partners in a downtown pool hall in the late 1930s. As soon as the pool room opened early Sunday morning, Wisehart was among the first town beer guzzlers to barge in.

On this particular Sunday, the regulars had gone through a keg by mid-morning. Brockwell brought out another and prepared to pull out the cork. Wisehart — the helpful servant — insisted that the honor for uncapping the new keg should belong to him.

Brockwell often said that 20/20 hindsight escaped him that day and he allowed Wes to take hold of the keg. Seems Wisehart lost his grip or stumbled and the full keg hit the floor. Brockwell recalled that foaming beer was forming in puddles.

Brockwell has wished a hundred times since that he had simply ushered his customers away and mopped up the beer. But any good bartender has this thing about letting good beer go to waste, and Jack didn't want to violate the code.

So he assisted as the concerned drunks scooped up the spilled beer in buckets, cans or any utensil available. That still amounted to a lot of beer, which his customers downed fast to prevent the embarrassment of being caught drinking stale beer.

Jack recalls that the salvaged beer was completely drank just a few minutes before noon, the time that the First Presbyterian preacher across the street dismissed his congregation. Brockwell said that, to his horror, he looked out and saw Wisehart and other drunks staggering from his pool room. Some were cussing, urinating against the building, and doing the unconscious things people do when having one too many.

The timing couldn't have been worse, recalled Brockwell. Across the street, the congregation, dressed in their Sunday best, were witnessing the same sin their preacher had cautioned against.

In no time, Paris Police Chief Earn Butler began receiving floods of angry calls from the upset church goers.

Then Butler contacted Brockwell and laid down an edict that applies to this day. "There'll be no more beer sold on Sunday, Jack."

Even putting on the badge of the law after being elected constable failed to separate Wisehart from controversy. In the 1940s when Paris — like the entire South — lawfully segregated the white and black races, Wisehart was angered when he saw a colored man seated on a courthouse bench reserved for whites.

He confronted the man and the black stabbed him with a screwdriver. Now angered to the point of killing the other, Wisehart pulled out his pistol. The scared colored man ran across the street — dodging traffic — and darted into Ezell & Douglas, a combination beer tavern and sports store. All the while, Wes was firing his gun as pedestrians scrambled for dear life.

The store also had a back room reserved for colored patrons, where the black man took refuge. Wisehart rushed the section, but his assailant was long gone into the streets.

One of the most controversial stories told about Wisehart occurred during his last years. A few years after Kentucky Lake was created from a dam built on the Tennessee River, duck hunting gained popularity in the Paris-Camden area. Wisehart, always one to make an easy buck, was suspected by many duck hunters of snatching their decoys from the water and selling them to other hunters.

Wisehart also had a favorite blind he liked to occupy during duck season. On one particular day, Wisehart steered a small motorboat to the blind and found that four soldiers from Fort Campbell, Ky., were homesteading the blind.

Wisehart yelled to them to leave "his blind." The soldiers laughed. Not taking Wisehart seriously nearly cost them their lives. Wisehart left and returned later with a can filled with gasoline. He poured the gasoline on the wood and brush blind and threw on a lighted match. The soldiers jumped into the lake for dear life, as the blind was enveloped in flames.

Most of the old timers who lived in Wisehart's reckless years are dead, disabled, or moved to other areas. But the wild life of Wes has been told and retold so many times, the character may outlive Porter, Harris, and Crockett.

Viola and 57 Students
Had One Dipper

Viola Carpenter and the 57 children she taught at one-teacher Eagle School in the years of the Great Depression had more than just the three R's in common. They drank spring water from the school's only dipper.

The dipper and bucket used to tote water from a nearby creek was one of the perks issued each year by the Lawrence County board of education. The school board — with the blessings of the county court — also "generously" gave the school two boxes of blackboard chalk and a few erasers to last for the eight-month term.

With no electricity to plug in even an antique fan, the students from the primmer through eighth grade sweated uncomfortably on sultry August days. The school term began early to make up for time lost through September and part of October, when schools closed for cotton picking.

And the winters — which were much colder in Tennessee then — taxed the single wood heating stove.

Teachers in the uncertain Depression years were fortunate if they made $50 a month, and much of her salary went toward paying room and board.

She also paid one of her students a buffalo nickel for getting up early and building a fire in the stove. She recalls that some of her pupils walked more than two miles from their rural homes to school. There was also a problem with some fathers of older boys, who felt their children would be just as well-learned by staying home to help during spring planting.

In 1935-36, Viola was merely one of many teachers in the South who dedicated themselves to seeing that rural children received at least an eighth grade education. There were times when she walked for miles — climbing steep ridges and fording creeks — to try and persuade stubborn farmers to keep their children in school, rather than at home, helping with crops.

"This was the period of home visits which teachers were required to make," she said. "One good thing about this … I had the chance to visit and spend a night or two with a cousin who lived close to the school."

While the school year was shorter than it is now, she recalls there were no snow days. "We'd walk through eleven inches of snow and sometimes more. But school continued on," she said.

Fortunately for Viola, she boarded with a kind family who lived adjacent to the school. "Their name was Hendrix, and like other families in the community, they did everything possible to help the school. Mrs. Hendrix even brought me a sack lunch each day at noon," she remembers.

Despite the ill-fated times, Viola recalls that the student body was almost universally united. "The more gifted, older students were good about helping the younger kids learn. One advantage of having the eight grades lumped together was that the younger children could learn in advance when they heard me teaching the seventh and eighth graders.

"Oh, I'm sure some of the parents today, who have no idea about what life was like in the Depression would rebel at the thought of one-room schools and everybody drinking water from the same dipper. But we did all right with the times, because most all the country kids came from homes without luxury or money to spend."

"Generations today — even the farm population — find it hard to comprehend that schools all over the South closed six weeks for cotton picking. The answer is very simple ... cotton was the top money crop and besides boosting the economy, cotton was the only way that boys and girls could have new clothes and shoes."

"It's ironic ... some teenagers today whine and fuss at their parents because their dress or coat is less expensive than the Jones' kids. We didn't have that temper tantrum in the Depression. Everybody was in the same boat, and all poor folks."

For sure, Eagle One-Teacher School was not allowed to turn in a budget for baseball bats and other sports equipment. But under the caring guidance of their teacher, they nevertheless enjoyed games like ring-around-the-rosie and drop the handkerchief at recess. The children also enjoyed the competitive game of town ball, in which bats were carved from tree limbs, which were plentiful.

Viola remembers that most of the children brought gallon tin buckets for lunch. Those buckets contained such food as ham sandwiches, jelly sandwiches, a baked potato, or sausage and biscuits.

In addition to emphasis on reading, writing and arithmetic, the teacher required students to memorize poems and held frequent spelling bees to help preserve the pupils' memory span.

With less than a token of contributions from a cash-strapped board of education, Viola set periodic box suppers to help raise money to purchase supplies.

Boys would ante up what currency they could muster, hoping to outbid rivals at auctions for articles donated by their favorite girl friend. "To the boy, it was a means of winning over his favorite girl friend, if he could outbid others for cookies that were made by that 'special' girl," Viola mused.

Mrs. Carpenter is convinced that children in today's pampered world are robbed of the opportunity to acquire good citizenship and Christian morals because of mandates by liberal federal judges.

"I am thankful that we had the freedom to pray and have Bible reading each morning before class. We also sang patriotic songs. It's so sad that children are denied the chance to voice their religious convictions these days," she said.

Mrs. Carpenter was issued a special teaching certificate in 1935, although she had completed but one year at Martin College in Pulaski.

"We had to spread our teacher training out over the years because we didn't have the money to afford four years of continuous tuition. But eventually, I was able to graduate at Middle Tennessee State College."

Her reward for teaching one-room Eagle School was a promotion to two-teacher Crews Town Grammar School.

If Viola's day was made easier because of an additional teacher to share the load, someone forgot to clue her in. "The children at Crews Town had the benefit of hot lunches. But the other teacher and I did the cooking, dish washing and cleaning," she explained.

Nevertheless, the parents also contributed, as each child attending Crews Town was required to bring his or her own bowl. The school also had the benefit of donated surplus butter, vegetables and other staples such as salt and pepper. Like their grown-ups, the students usually satisfied themselves with such helpings as soup beans and ground cold carrots mixed with raisins.

Before retiring in 1978, Mrs. Carpenter taught in various other smaller schools in the county, including Etheridge Graded School. She later taught 13 years at West Highland Elementary in her native Lawrenceburg.

Her roots venture back to the early 1800s and many of her ancestors were acquainted with David Crockett, whose political career began when he was elected the first mayor of Lawrenceburg. Among her ancestors who helped pioneer the county was John Allen, who operated a cotton and grist mill.

Extremely proud of the county's heritage, she has fought more than one battle to save historic homes and other landmarks.

"A lot of us got after some of the politicians for tearing down the old courthouse, but they did it in spite of how most folks felt," she said.

She married Charles Edward Carpenter and they had four children. One of them, Margaret Ann Wolfe, followed her mother's career pursuit, now teaching in the state of Virginia.

A real history buff, Mrs. Carpenter has seldom been idle since leaving education. Her community frequently beckons and Viola is only happy to respond to the city, which she thinks has the greatest people in the world.

She contributed to historical projects in Tennessee Homecoming — 1986 and again in the 1996 state bicentennial.

The Mountain's Tough
Prosecutor

They know him as the gutsy district attorney who drove the St. Louis mob out of Newport. He ranks high among Tennessee District Attorneys General ... he may be tops.

But for Al Schmutzer, one of his biggest battles was in just getting an opportunity to take his case before the highest tribunal of all, the people.

When Schmutzer decided to give up a good law practice in his native Sevierville in 1974 to run for District Attorney General, he learned he wasn't the favorite of the small but powerful Republican political clique. For decades a so-called nominating committee of about seven power bosses had handpicked the candidate for offices like circuit judge and attorney general. In the near solid GOP district this was tantamount to election.

The machine received it's first severe jolt when State Sen. Kenneth Porter sued for an open primary. Porter won his suit and proceeded to trounce longtime incumbent Judge George Shepherd.

Schmutzer had already made up his mind to run as an independent, a decision not always without risk in Republican mountain strongholds, where staunch party loyalists view independents as warmed over Democrats.

Schmutzer assured voters that he came from a staunch Republican family and was running independent only because the machine was robbing the people of their options. Schmutzer whipped the incumbent, who was a willing tool of machine politics, mountain style.

Schmutzer, as much as Porter, deserved credit for ending one of the state's last machines. He proved that whether by open primary or the independent route, people were fed to the gills with boss rule.

But the young attorney's struggles had just begun. He campaigned on a pledge to bring an end to the growing truck stop prostitution ring which was causing the moonshine-plagued county it's greatest shame.

Even with the busy truck traffic on Interstate 40, the independent-natured mountain folks had to wonder about new truck stops going up on every entrance highway into the city. They were more surprised when sexy sounding young women — many with distinctive Northern accents — got on CB radios and invited weary truckers to stop in for a $50 cup of coffee.

Whether or not to let the out-of-state Mafia build a thriving illegal truck stop prostitution ring in his district was the immediate task facing the newly-elected attorney general, a graduate of the University of the South and former FBI agent.

Newport and Cocke County was already known as the moonshine capital of the world. In recent years, many people who didn't exactly fret about breaking the law had turned to the lucrative trade of growing marijuana.

Also, decent folks who liked to live right and walk straight had reason to doubt the sincerity of their law enforcement. Although the county was dry, the county's hundreds of taverns and joints sold bootleg whiskey like wildfire, whether to drink on the premises or carry home.

Contrary to state law — which called for an end to the sale of beer by midnight and a ban on Sunday sales — tavern operators freely established their own hours. Sometimes, taverns went full swing all night. Poker, slot machines, dice shooting, cockfighting, and other forms of gambling were rampant.

Amusing was the tendency of some of the hardened beer and moonshine drinkers at Cosby to unzip their trousers — oblivious to passing motorists — and place bets on who could piss the furthest, next furthest, and so on.

Everyone but everyone drew their own conclusions: that the law was certainly taking kickbacks. More pronounced was that many of the tavern owners poured money behind the candidate for sheriff they felt would best suit their interests.

Moonshining had more or less been regarded as a necessity in Cocke County. The rugged nature of the mountainous land and steep ridges all but made it impossible for the average man to feed his family by farming. To make it in factories, less fortunate people had to commute to Knoxville, Morristown, and other cities for work.

Even federal tax agents who were dedicated to dent the moonshine industry sometimes did not pursue hard-pressed whiskey makers, once their still was destroyed.

But truck stop prostitution — even involving girls as young as fifteen — that was different. Besides, the truck stop ring was masterminded by a racketeering mob in St. Louis-East St. Louis, Illinois, headed by the Robinson Brothers.

The new district attorney had no time to kill ... the multimillion dollar illegal industry was already full steam ahead. But neither did Schmutzer take a Florida vacation to celebrate his election victory.

By the time he took office, Schmutzer had learned the tricks of the mob. "They were cunning and experienced pros," said Schmutzer.

"A truck driver, to get into back rooms with a girl, had to show his commercial driver's license. It was strictly cash and carry ...they did not need scrutiny from the IRS.

"The hired prostitutes did not stay long in Newport, but were replaced within three days by other girls who were shuttled between cities. The mob also took every guarantee to see that their prostitutes wouldn't be caught in violation of the Mann Act," he explained.

Schmutzer's years in the FBI, where he learned undercover work, proved to be an ace in the hole in his war against the mob. Some of his agents were actually planted behind wheels of 18-wheeler trucks. They were perfect clones for hard living, free drinking drivers, and even carried on the routine of telling dirty jokes.

By the same token, Schmutzer ordered complete radio silence knowing that the truck stop operators had scanners. Neither did he broadcast his movements to local law enforcement, aware that a dishonest cop might tip off the mob.

In no time, Schmutzer had conducted a raid and made arrests. He quickly padlocked the business which, by state law, was effective for up to four months. As the fiery DA raided another and still another illegal truck stop, it was obvious those businesses were out for the duration.

The raids also brought out the wrath of the St. Louis mob. The Robinson Brothers, who were engaged in multimillion dollar prostitution rings, never intended to be driven from their Southern base by a hillbilly prosecutor.

The operation had reached the point of no return to their point of view. Shortly, Schmutzer was informed by the FBI that a $20,000 contract was put out to eliminate him.

Schmutzer's precarious predicament was all the more risky when he realized that murder contracts were issued in Cocke County for as little as $500.

Already there were grumblings by tavern hoppers about this upstart 'general' from Sevierville, trying to spoil their fun. Would the mob's quest to do in Schmutzer be made easier by finding a confederate in the hills?

The FBI had also learned that Alex Evolga, who lived in Cincinnati, Ohio and had a connections with the Robinsons, was in on the murder for hire contract.

Not only did Evolga have ties in Newport, he had every reason for revenge against the DA. Months before, Schmutzer had prosecuted Evolga who was accused in the murder of the Irish Cut Tavern owner in Newport. Evolga was convicted and appealed.

The conviction was overturned by an appeals judge on what Schmutzer termed "another scared witness syndrome in the mountains."

After the shooting of the tavern operator, two witnesses volunteered that they watched the murder. One of the witnesses was frightened off from giving initial testimony, but the other's testimony was enough to convince a jury.

The witness changed his testimony at the second trial, and Schmutzer suspected mob intimidation.

Weeks later, Evolga was charged in a drug deal down in Florida and sentenced to prison. Later paroled, Evolga was bent on destroying the DA.

Through informants in the St. Louis-Chicago area, the FBI learned the identity of the hit man. Former prison inmate Junior Lester Lee, who was known in Newport and Knoxville, was paid $10,000 in advance to carry out the contract. Once fulfilled, Lee was to receive the remaining $10,000.

Schmutzer was warned to take extra precaution ... the FBI knew Lee was already headed South. With the DA's family and friends already concerned, near panic ensued in Sevierville, when a cabin retreat on the Little Pigeon River where the Schmutzers sometimes stayed, burned mysteriously.

Rumors that the mob had sought to harm Schmutzer by burning the cabin circulated around favorite morning coffee drinking places in Sevierville, like Ellisons and Newman's Cafe.

Later, Schmutzer would discount arson, saying that the origin of the fire which destroyed the cabin — owned by his father — was undetermined.

An even greater scare came when neighbors of the Schmutzers saw a strange car with out-of-state license tags parked for a considerable time across from the Schmutzer home. The Schmutzers happened to be gone at the time.

The driver seen behind the wheel was described as dark complexioned and matching the appearance of Lee. Lee was also reported seen in Knoxville the afternoon before. Sevierville is about a 30 minute drive from Knoxville.

To Schmutzer's knowledge, the sighting of the mysterious car may have been the closest attempt on his life. With their pet East Tennessee operation already in shambles, the Robinsons apparently backed off, not wanting to bring further wrath against them by harming the hillbilly prosecutor who dared to fight for principle.

The end of the truck stop prostitution case was hardly closed when Schmutzer received another jolt. On Christmas Day, 1976 he was awakened at 3:20 a.m. by a ringing telephone. There had been many shots fired in the Red Lantern Tavern on Highway 25 West in Newport. Four people were dead.

The deadly assault had been engineered by Rusty Dallas Denton, a hard-living young man in his early twenties. Denton, whose father was rich, prominent, and politically powerful in the community, apparently acted out of revenge.

The viciousness of the attack — which spoiled Christmas for several families — was evidenced when Denton chased one of the wounded victims to the parking lot before killing him. To make certain the man was dead, Denton ran over the victim's body with his automobile.

Based on previous killings which involved prominent families, the betting man would have given good odds that Denton would not serve a day for the violent crime. Schmutzer, knowing that jurors have often been intimidated in high velocity mountain cases, may have had doubts himself.

However, to the attorney general's delight, the trial judge protected the jury from public view, at the same time telling them they could become heroes by finally bringing justice to the mountains.

Denton was convicted and sentenced to life, but the book on the Red Lantern killings was far from closed. Early in January, 1980, as Governor Ray Blanton was in the last days of his term, a major scandal was surfacing in Nashville.

Blanton, a former West Tennessee congressman, was rumored to be accepting thousands of dollars in bribes for granting paroles to felons in the state penitentiary in Nashville. Some felons he paroled were among the most dangerous men behind prison walls.

Blanton was bitterly criticized shortly after Christmas, 1979, when he pardoned Roger Humphries, who had been found guilty in the murder of his estranged wife and her boyfriend in Johnson City. Humphries' father was a political supporter of Blanton.

The pardon led to House Speaker Ned Ray McWherter's getting Governor-elect Lamar Alexander, a Maryville Republican, sworn in three days early. McWherter, like Blanton a Democrat, feared that at least 100 more pardons might be extended by Blanton.

One of the felons who Blanton was expected to release was Denton. There was a report that $25,000 had been given to Blanton for Denton's freedom.

Denton's ability to move about Newport taverns was apparently quashed by the big man from Weakley County who would himself become governor eight years later.

The fast-moving DA would soon learn sadly that not all was good in booming Sevier County, where the never-ending tourist dollar had made instant millionaires of friends. With prosperity and legitimate businessmen came the scum of the earth from dark corners across the nation.

But it wasn't the bad Yankee import that caused the worst crime in the county's modern history ... the Kodak bank murders.

The warm sunny morning before Easter Sunday, 1977 found a cheerful Earl Underwood entering the mobile home off State Highway 66 that temporarily housed a branch of Citizens National Bank. The community's first bank, it was located two miles from I-40.

Underwood, a retired Air Force Major, was a magistrate on the Sevier County Court. A staunch fiscal conservative, he was respected by constituents as a watchdog for the community.

Underwood could not know that he was about to walk in on an armed holdup. Inside were George Brady and Leroy Marshall. The holdup men, both brandishing pistols, lived in Newport. Held at bay were three bank employees.

It has been speculated that Underwood must have recognized Brady, a Sevier County native who had once done some work at Underwood's home. Whether Underwood's recognition of Brady was the ensuing factor in the brutal murders will never be known.

The four — two men and two women — were forced to lie face down in the small drive-in teller compartment and riddled with bullets fired from close range.

The violent act, by two petty hoods who were known to be heavy drug users and gamblers, stunned the county. Also, there was the rude awakening that terror rode the interstate and the area's quiet, easy going reputation was forever gone.

Ironically, Gov. Blanton had vetoed a bill in the General Assembly to restore Tennessee's new death penalty only a week before the Kodak murders. Although the Kodak killers escaped capital punishment, they were sentenced to a total of 412 years in federal prison.

Schmutzer has been called on to prosecute numerous other murders in Sevier County alone. Senseless killings — like the fatal shooting of young Gatlinburg policeman Donnie Huskey, who was attempting to arrest a young man, who was high on drugs.

Early in the 1980s, two Kentucky teenagers were strangled in a Gatlinburg hotel. The double murders, the first in the resort's history, hit the city's pulse rate hard.

Still a more gruesome twin killing would occur at the Rocky Top Motel at Gatlinburg. The business was owned by Beaudeaux and Felicia Bryant, coauthors of the hit song Rocky Top.

Savagely murdered were a female desk clerk and a security guard. One of the men convicted was Eddie "Tattoo" Harris, who received the death penalty.

Harris was regarded as an extremely dangerous misfit with no regard for human life.

Pigeon Forge, which has become one of the South's fastest-growing resorts, was also in line for violence. The city's shock came when a prominent business-woman was found brutally slain. Two persons, one a 14-year-old girl, were convicted. They had, among other insults, drank the victim's blood.

Unlike Harris, the youthful killers were members of native Sevier County families.

Another double killing, which also involved suspects who were native countians, took place in Sevier and neighboring Blount counties. The killers, Dellinger and Sutton, first killed a man in Blount County, and later surprised the victim's sister, who was searching for her brother's body in Sevier County. The unfortunate woman was slain and her car burned with her remains inside.

Perhaps the most emotionally draining case for Schmutzer was the November, 1994 murder of Kelly Lavera. Lavera was bludgeoned to death by Brett Rae. Rae and Lavera's widow, Shane Mills Lavera, were charged, convicted of first degree murder, and sentenced to 25 years, with no chance of parole.

Rae was accused of beating Kelly Lavera to death with his son's baseball bat so that Rae could continue a romantic relationship with Lavera's wife, Shane. After Lavera was beaten unconscious, Rae loaded the body into the victim's jeep and ran it over a steep cliff near Gatlinburg to make it appear Lavera died in an accident.

Suspicion of Shane Lavera's involvement intensified when Sevierville Chief of Police Robbie Fox discovered blood on the living room carpet of the Lavera's apartment.

Schmutzer gradually built his case against the defendants with the cooperation of both relatives and close friends of Mrs. Lavera and Rae, who had turned state witnesses.

The case was far from easy for Schmutzer and Sevier County authorities because Mrs. Lavera was the daughter of popular Gatlinburg socialites, the late Brent Mills and Sandy Mills. Brent Mills was the only son of longtime Gatlinburg Mayor Bill Mills, founder of First National Bank.

After the elder Mills died, his son became president of the bank. The bank was believed one of the most solvent in East Tennessee, while under the guidance of the no-nonsense former mayor.

However, the bank fell on hard times, apparently because of Brent Mills' lax policy in granting loans. He died of a self-inflicted gun wound hours before bank examiners were to conduct an audit.

Rae was the son of Rick Rae, a Canadian native who was hired as publisher of a troubled Sevier County newspaper owned by Harte-Hanks.

The years of courtroom pain have taken a toll on Schmutzer, even though he appears as brilliant as ever. Soon, he will wrestle with his greatest decision of all time: whether to make a second run for First District Congress in 1998, or vie for another eight-year term as attorney general.

Schmutzer, who has never been challenged for reelection as DA, was narrowly defeated in the congressional race two years ago, to fill the vacant seat left by the retirement of legendary Jimmie Quillen. However, Schmutzer had the satisfaction of carrying his native county by polling about 95 percent of the vote.

However, Schmutzer was eased out by Congressman Bill Jenkins who got a major portion of the big vote-rich Tri-Cities area of Upper East Tennessee.

Regardless of the DA's eventual decision, he will leave a giant mark in the annuls of mountain justice … as the right man who came forth at just the right time.

Wash Tub Good Mode of Transportation in 17 Inch Snow

Retired school teacher Gladys Dixon has three pet peeves about modern education.

She can never get used to empty school houses when it snows in the hollers. She believes that modern day educators are too free in spending the taxpayers' money by being in the transportation business.

And Gladys — who married Horace Dixon — just cannot accept today's pampered teachers in heavy makeup, who spend as much time whining for more money as they do worrying about where Johnny got that marijuana cigarette.

It was 1934 when the gracious lady landed her first teaching job at Boogertown School in the mountains of Sevier County. She taught the 3 R's, swept the floor, chased the bears away, and put out the wampus cat, before walking the two miles to her home, if that was the only transportation.

For all this and more, Mrs. Dixon earned $60 a month, but had to pay some of that to have fires built in the wood stove on cold days.

On one of those really cold days in the mountains, Gladys woke up to 17 inches of snow. There wasn't a sign of the narrow dirt road leading by the school, although it had been visible the night before.

The lady had to put on some high boots and lots of warm clothes before starting down the road. It was before morning light and pitch dark when she heard some sort of commotion and little children laughing behind her.

She brushed the caked snow from her face and was rather startled to see a grown man pulling a wash tub with a rope. Two children rode in the tub and at least two more kids walked behind the tub.

That tub was not only transportation for the children, but also a snowplow opening the road to school. On this particular morning, Gladys didn't wade into her usual early morning routine of teaching reading and arithmetic. First, she had to warm pans of water to soothe the nearly frostbitten hands of students who had walked the furthest.

Next, she spent the better part of an hour placing wet shoes, caps, and coats near the warm morning heater for drying. Then Gladys Dixon got around to teaching reading, writing, arithmetic, spelling, Tennessee history, and something called discipline, which seems to be missing from many of today's bigger, consolidated schools.

Before that, however, Gladys opened with prayer, devotion, and patriotic songs like *Dixie* and *America.*

That's another pet peeve with Gladys: The federal government and its liberal judges have outlawed school prayer. The lady just can't understand.

Today, the government insists that children eat certain so-called balanced diets, but Horace and Gladys and other taxpayers are sent the bill.

"Lord ... I can see even now my little school children sitting on the school house steps or under trees eating dinner, and it was just about always ham or sausage and biscuits stacked in lard cans. Once and awhile, some mothers would throw in a baked potato or boiled ear of corn for good measure," Gladys recalled.

And how dedicated was Gladys? Well, former educator Frank Marshall, in his after dinner talks, frequently marveled how Gladys taught the 3 R's to him - a kid who all other teachers had given up on.

What's more, the boy seemed bent on refusing to learn. Gladys learned that the lad loved to fish and that that's how she approached his interest.

With Gladys' tutoring, the lad was soon catching trout, notties, and all kinds of fish in his wildest daydreams. The lady teacher also mastered new words and picked up sounds associated with fishing. Not bad for a teacher who started teaching with two years at Mars Hill Junior College.

Some of her old students at Boogertown went on to be quite successful, too. Among them ... Clyde Blalock, Woody and Donald Brackins, Preacher W.W. Cope and her niece, Betty D. Gillette.

Montgomery

For Sevier County to be without a Montgomery upholding the law would be akin to the Bible without the New Testament.

You might say that former state legislator B.B. Montgomery started a proud tradition when he doubled as physician and respected mediator at primitive Elkmont Lumber Camp in the wild 1920s.

In the years since, he's had a son and two grandsons who have laid down the law in the best and worst years of Sevier County. Their community couldn't be happier.

Wallace Montgomery was a member of the Gatlinburg police force going back to when it was a two man operation.

I knew Wall in later years as the resort mecca in the Smoky Mountains mushroomed and he was elevated to assistant chief. Probably one of the best compliments I ever heard about Wall was from a successful Gatlinburg business-man. "If Mr. Wall hadn't literally spanked our butts and lectured us in the fear of God when we did a lot of foolish things, where would we be today?"

Wallace Montgomery indeed had earned respect and they say he would walk a mile to help a wayward boy to walk the narrow path if he could.

But Montgomery — who served under Chief Wib Ogle during the years when the department was becoming one of the state's most disciplined — wouldn't be hesitant to face the devil in a tunnel with no lights if the devil needed arresting.

I've heard this same businessman say that "Mr. Wall will back down to no man."

Wallace has two sons who ably followed in their dad's footsteps. Bruce, his older son, had an outstanding, long career as federal Marshall, serving under Presidents Gerald Ford, Jimmy Carter, Ronald Reagan, and George Bush.

Like his father and grandfather, Bruce Montgomery exemplified the warmth that aroused a felon's feelings, but with a firmness that humbled the most-hardened of bad men.

I once heard a moonshiner say that if I ever have to walk that last few feet to the penitentiary again, I hope that Bruce Montgomery is showing me the way."

Montgomery is the high sheriff of Sevier County and I'm forever hearing the words "firm, but fair." A levelheaded administrator, folks in East Tennessee say he can keep the job as long as he wants.

He's no hard-nosed Buford Pusser, but his ability as a good administrator is getting statewide publicity just the same.

I recall Sheriff Leon Williams of Henry County say that "each time I go to the mountains, I learn something new from Bruce."

And Williams is the efficient lawman who engineered the quality security patrol at Land Between the Lakes.

Harry Montgomery is remembered throughout the state as the outstanding athlete at Pi Beta Phi High School in the 1950s who led the TSSAA scoring in both football and basketball the same year.

It's a record that still stands, but as Chief of Police for the Gatlinburg Police Department, Harry's record for heading a police force in one of the state's most difficult cities has also drawn state scrutiny.

Harry had his troubles a few years ago because he couldn't hold his drink. He may owe his life — certainly as a lawmen — to his dad. More than once, Wallace Montgomery walked in to take home his son, when no one else dared.

Harry became a successful police officer when he realized there are some forces you can't beat down. That's when he gave up John Barleycorn.

Harry tried for sheriff in 1978 and lost; on the other hand, Bruce lost his first race too. Whether Harry may try again when his older brother steps down is fuel for speculation in the mountains.

Definitely, Tennessee's most famous law enforcement family is hopeful that Harry's only son will keep alive the tradition started by his great grandfather B.B.

Definitely, law abiding citizens everywhere will be better if the circle continues.

Ramp Eating Hillbillies

Y ou don't have to leave theVolunteer State to find people who never tasted a ramp. Go to Clarksville or Paris and they'll say a ramp is something you drive a truck on. But in the courthouses at Maryville, Newport, Sevierville ... those ramps can get mighty smelly.

Actually, it's surprising that ramps are still so much of a secret on the other end of Tennessee and in the other 49 states. In the late 1940s, the Cosby Ruritans — perhaps wishing to see their area get a more positive reputation than as a moonshine capital — organized the Ramp Festival.

Harry S. Truman, when he was president, attracted 100,000 people to the one-day celebration held high on a beautiful mountain. So did Bob Hope.

The ramp festival is still held the first Sunday in May, although the site has shifted closer to Newport. The promoters usually draw some headline country music stars from the Grand Ole Opry, but old timers around Cosby say there will never be a crowd like those that went to see Hope and Truman.

Still, there are a few thousand fans who spend the day taking in mountain entertainment and eating fried cornbread, chicken and of course potatoes cooked in ramps. The highlight of the day is the crowning of the Ramp Queen, who traditionally received a hug and a kiss from Congressman Jimmie Quillen.

Cooked in Irish potatoes or scrambled eggs, ramps are tasty, but that won't buy you the time of day from a real ramp-eating hillbilly son-of-a-gun.

Eat a dozen or so raw ramps, right after they are picked from high in the mountains, and you have a weapon comparable to a scud missile. Ramps — which are cultivated in March or very early spring — may resemble garlic or onions in taste.

But raw ramps are guaranteed to keep away the bill collector and may even have the wife kicking you into the dog house for weeks at a time.

Ramps have been a treasured custom in the Smoky Mountains of East Tennessee for longer than anyone knows. Even before the February snows start to melt, hillbillies are climbing at least 1,200 feet to stake their claim. The late Dick McNabb may have been the best ramp digger in Sevier County.

Dick would get up early on a cold morning and hike further up than the typical ramp eater. He'd make a day of it, taking corn meal and sacks for the ramps. He had favorite spots all over the mountains. Somewhere along the way, McNabb and his friends would stop and cook some of that great fried skillet cornbread and potatoes, laced in ramps.

One thing you never saw McNabb take in the mountains was a skillet and cooking utensils. He had them buried all over the mountains. After raking into the snow — should he find a healthy patch — he'd spot a familiar beech tree or rock formation. He'd step off four or five paces and start digging. The skillet and pots were exactly where he buried them, one, two ... maybe five years before.

Dick and his friends would sit about a warm fire, eating and chasing with moonshine or Jim Beam. Then the hillbillies would dig into the snow to get possibly the first batch of ramps of the new season.

McNabb said that ramps had a better — more potent — taste when picked before the snow disappeared.

He once described them as frisky, like a mean rattler when his hibernation is prematurely disturbed.

Aaron (Big A) Kirby used to walk or hitch a ride from his shack in a Chincapin holler to Sevierville 20 miles distant to sit around the courthouse and swap knives. But Big A's business dropped during ramp season. That's because the lawyers and Yankee tourists couldn't get too near.

Pless Newman was a powerful Republican politician in his day, compared with boss Ed Crump when it came to getting his kinfolks and friends elected to office. During ramp season, folks walking into trial justice court used to gag after a whiff from Pless' mouth. Not everybody of course ... Pless always had a passel of friends coming to ask for favors. They, too, had got up that morning, smacking on raw ramps.

I use to enjoy hearing Pless explain the ramp tradition to those Yankee tourists who were nearly overcome by the odor. Newman's familiar line was this: "We mountain people were raised on ramps and so was our great pappaws. It's a slight onion ... only sweeter and more tender. It grows well at mountain elevations and does very well in damp, acid soil, especially in white oak tracts. It has a most persistent, lingering odor that can turn away bill collectors and even politicians who don't indulge. It has been known to intensify in great abundance when mixed with moonshine drink stilled in our mountains."

While it takes the hardy and carefree like Pless and Big A to get on raw ramp eating binges, tasty ramp-cooking recipes have been passed down among mountain families for ages. A dish of fried ramps alone has boosted the morale of poor mountaineers for many generations.

The younger generation, though, tends to draw the line by frying a tad of ramps in fried potatoes or scrambled in eggs. That's what you get at the ramp festival. Or, better still, at the supper tables of hillbillies like Dale Bradshaw, W.H. Ogle and Donald Dodgen.

Preacher Rogers

At a time when Sunday church attendance is taking a downturn, Preacher Paul Rogers is packing them in as he begins his 42nd year at Centerville Church of Christ.

You might say Preacher Paul has a total package for his 850-member congregation. In the years the Alabama native has been pastor, average church attendance has grown from 350 to 650, and annual contributions to carry on the Lord's work have increased from $19,000 to $490,000.

The reason for the unusual, high attendance is best exemplified by one particular family. That family drives 50 miles each way, every Sunday, to hear Preacher Rogers preach the Bible. And what is most remarkable is that Hickman County has 42 Church of Christ congregations and Centerville has a population of just 4,000.

Further test of Rogers' ability to perform miracles is that under his leadership, the congregation has built a beautiful new church and popular summer youth camp. Camp Meribatt, high over the scenic Duck River, across Highway 100, attracts youth from miles away. The camp is valued at $250,000.

In keeping with Preacher Rogers' master plan to have something nice for all, the church complex has constructed a $2,500,000, five-story apartment complex for senior citizens, appropriately called Tulipwood. In addition, there is a $200,000 outreach center for benevolence and senior citizen work.

A newer project which benefits the entire community and all religious faiths, is a $1,200,000 educational and fellowship complex. More than 100 preschool children are enrolled under tutelage of qualified teachers.

Rogers, indeed, has become a powerful influence in the community, since moving there from Birmingham Jan. 1, 1967. However, if you plan to drive a long distance just to meet the man, call first. Rogers has toured the world doing the Lord's work and is ever available for the calling.

In 1963, he was away in London, England, campaigning for the Lord. In

1969, he went to Israel where he studied archaeology and was continuing the good work for the church.

He was preaching over in India in 1975 and preached tirelessly behind the Iron Curtain in Russia two years later. In addition, the preacher has visited the Holy Land on three occasions and frequently carried the message to Turkey and the Cacaos Islands.

The stout gentleman has spoken on lectureships at more universities than most bearers of God's word could dream about. Those universities include Harding Graduate School of Religion where he earned his M.A. degree, and David Lipscomb, where he received his bachelor. He serves on the board of Lipscomb, where he's also secretary of the Johnson Scholarship Foundation.

His importance to the Centerville community is awesome. He didn't get off the cabbage truck yesterday, either, serving as the very first president of Centerville Elementary P.T.A.

His fierce community involvement also includes being past chairman of the Hickman County library board; chairing the Centerville Beautiful Commission; and a member of the city's industrial board. He's also on the board at First Farmer's and Merchant's Bank.

The remarkable preacher — who has conducted more than 700 funerals in the county — has been awarded numerous honors, including honorary membership in the Jaycees, for his community service.

One of his proudest moments of all came in 1978, when Rogers was voted Centerville Man of the Year. Another milestone happened when the Tennessee General Assembly honored him with a resolution in 1983, citing his long ministry and community service.

Brother Rogers' life and unrelenting philosophy is further immortalized in his autobiography, *These 40 Years ... the best of four decades in one pulpit.*

Explaining his fascination with preaching, he blended blunt admission with Minnie Pearl type homespun humor,

He said: "I have been loved by almost everybody and loathed by a few. I have been helped by the many, heckled by a few."

He knows exactly where Winston Churchill was coming from when the great World War II Prime Minister related, "There is no more exhilarating feeling on earth than to be shot at without result."

When one citizen in Centerville compared Rogers with a barking dog, the slur was immediately countered by the elderly lady who publicly said Rogers was the greatest preacher she ever heard. "I knew then that the truth lay somewhere in between those two extremes," he chuckled.

And indeed, traveling around the globe can bring confusion. Once, he was asked if he was Billy Graham. Another time, an airline stewardess mistook him for Paul Harvey.

And then there is the cold hard reality of life. Once, he cosigned a bank note for a friend and ended up having to pay it off. He received a letter one day, in which the writer threatened to blow up the church and shoot the preacher's head off.

Still, Rogers likes to preach and wouldn't have it any other way.

He is convinced that it takes more raw courage to stand in the pulpit than enter a boxing ring with a Jack Dempsey.

Big Apple

Tennessee Highway patrolmen Wayne Tubbs and Robert Earl Melton responded to what surely was another boring routine call at the Big Apple Club near Puryear.

The nightclub — known for it's good food like Southern barbecue — was popular hangout for Murray State University students. Since Murray, Ky. was a dry city, students flocked across the state line in Tennessee to down a few beers and let off steam.

The night of March 31, 1977 was a special night because it was the anniversary of the wet T-shirt party, a fad that only young college students, rebelling against authority, can appreciate.

Complaints had reached the Highway Patrol headquarters that many cars were parked on the shoulders of Highway 641, a state right of way.

The troopers went to the night club in their separate cars. Neither had the slightest idea it would be the most trying and potentially dangerous evening of their law enforcement careers.

Tubbs, who went on to retire from the THP in the mid-1980s with the rank of lieutenant, recalled that he entered the nightclub and announced that automobiles parked on the state right away violated state law and had to be immediately moved.

Just as quickly, one intoxicated student showed his rotten side and Tubbs arrested him for being intoxicated.

As the drunk student was being placed in Tubbs' cruiser, Candy, a loud

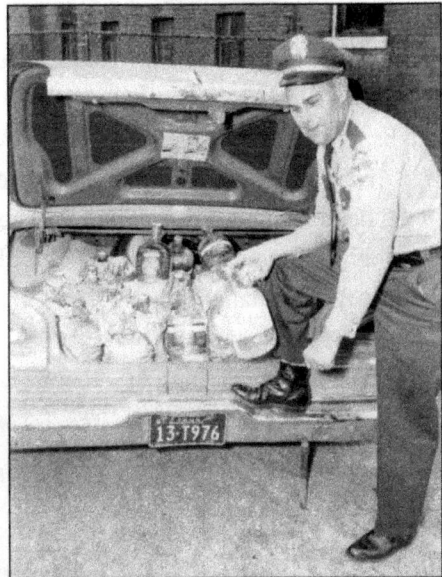

college girl who was screaming obscenities, demanded her fellow student be freed and allowed back inside.

Just as quickly, other students high on beer and brown-bagged liquor, poured outside and began throwing rocks at the THP cars. Tubbs later recalled saying, "we were in a lot of trouble that we never dreamed would have been possible in dealing with college students.

"I know now that at least one-half of the Murray State football team was in on the T-shirt party. They poured into the parking lot as if Robert Earl and I were their despised homecoming opponent.

"We knew that what would have ordinarily been a peaceful exercise of enforcing a minor infraction was becoming extremely dangerous," explained Tubbs.

Tubbs recalls that he barely hurried into his car as a beer bottle grazed him in the head. He quickly grabbed his shot gun and all the shells on hand. Sending a frantic radio transmission to District Highway Patrol headquarters in Jackson, Tubbs warned that a riot was taking place at the Big Apple in Puryear.

The troopers wisely parked their cruisers so that the vehicles blocked each

end of the circle driveway and other vehicles could not enter or exit the parking lot.

Tubbs then radioed an emergency for the entire Paris police department and county sheriff's department to speed to the Big Apple. Arriving promptly were local constables and the one-man Puryear police department.

Tubbs has always credited the quick response of local law enforcement units with averting further violence and possible death. "Our few deputies and police were still decidedly outnumbered by the T-shirt party people, but I believe,, to this day, their appearance saved the day, until troopers from Jackson, Brownsville and other places came in," said Tubbs.

Tubbs also gave much credit to Murray State head football coach, Bill Ferguson. "Bill drove as fast as he could from Murray … I honestly believe that he may have stopped some bloodletting.

"Those football players were roaring drunk and had kill on their minds. But when the coach showed up, they acted like timid house kittens," asserted Tubbs.

"The players had been drinking and mouthing off like they owned the world. You can imagine how they sobered up at the sight of their coach. I think they realized their scholarships and whole future was on the line."

As troopers sped in by the dozens, the fight seemed to have been taken out of all but a dozen of the nearly hundred college students who had only minutes before attempted to take the law by force.

One wet T-shirt advocate who proved an exception to law and order was Candy. Although handcuffed, she shouted obscenities and kicked in the back of the cruiser's window.

School buses were sent in at the request of Tubbs and a total of 202 students and cohorts were arrested and driven to Paris to face a judge.

Tubbs recalled that the judge really gave the students a blistering lecture about throwing away their education and future. About 20 were jailed on more serious charges.

The others were placed on bond and cited to appear for a court date. Tubbs believes that all but a handful forfeited bond and were happy to put the experience behind them. At least five who had committed more serious offenses like Candy were fined and given 11 months, 29-day jail sentences.

Tubbs has thanked his God ever since that some of the drunken T-shirt party goers didn't foolishly rush the shotgun-wielding troopers and get hurt because of their foolishness.

Tubbs said that if he learned one thing from the Big Apple riots, it was to never take even the most routine response to duty with a grain of salt.

To the careful observer, its inconceivable that a seemingly harmless T-shirt party by happy college students could overshadow the tense confrontations Tubbs faced in the wild years of moonshining and bootlegging in Henry County.

He recalled that real whiskey runners were capable of outsmarting any law. Like the day when Tubbs got after a whiskey runner between Paris and Dover.

"I searched that car with a fine tooth comb from front to back, over and over. I could see the smirk on this 'shiner's face … 'like, well I done outfoxed another lawman.'

"Then, as I was about to give it up, I remembered thinking it funny that the spare tire in the back of his truck was over inflated.

"I began to check and learned why it was over inflated: it was filled with white lightening."

There was also a day when he and a deputy working for the late Sheriff Alvis Wall, literally scrutinized the car of a suspected runner from the axles to the headliner.

They even took both seats out and found nothing, no secret compartments … nothing. Then, by gut reaction, they decided to have one final look at the rear seat. This time they pulled the stuffing apart, and there was the bonded booze.

Tubbs' outstanding record as a highway patrolman has outlasted retirement. Since he retired as a lieutenant, he has turned down offers originating at the governor's office to return and accept the rank of Captain.

In 1994 when Sheriff Leon Williams made a successful comeback after an absence of twenty-five years, he offered the job of chief deputy to Tubbs.

Tubbs, who has enjoyed working in security for mammoth Spinks Clay Co. in Routon for several years, politely turned down both job opportunities.

But the heart of the old country boy from Yuma in Carroll County will always remain in the highway patrol. He has also been influential in recruiting other fine officers into the THP, including popular Trooper David Bumpus.

A Boy Named Sue

Years ago country singer Johnny Cash got a lot of mileage out of a song he wrote titled "A Boy Named Sue." Other than Monroe County in Southeast Tennessee, not many people know there really was a boy named Sue.

In the 1960s, Cash was entertaining at a meeting of the Tennessee Trial Judges Association at Gatlinburg. The presiding judge that year was Sue Hicks of Madisonville. Before Cash returned to his home in Nashville, a new song was in the making. In a bar room, Cash's leading character met the "S.O.B. who give me that awful name of Sue."

The young man and his long wondering Pa wrestled and rolled in the mud, the blood, and the beer. The old man proved tough and bit off a piece of Sue's ear. The son got the better of the old man, but spared him when he learned why his Pa gave him that embarrassing name. His Pa, who had to be gone from home for months at a time to find work, assured his son that it was for the best.

"I knew you'd have to learn to be tough and I wouldn't be around."

The old man reasoned correctly that his boy would have to learn to whip several ruffians a day who were bound to tease him at length.

Judge Sue Hicks had been a partner in a one hundred year old law firm before running for and being elected criminal judge.

No doubt the years of being teased by peers influenced his years as judge. He ran a mighty tough court, as any number of unfortunate moonshiners, muggers, and other criminals found out.

Sue Hicks wasn't any easier on lawyers or news reporters. More than one whimpering big city lawyer limped back to Chattanooga after violating the rules in Hicks' court.

Dan Hicks, one of the few Tennessee journalist to receive the Quill award for courageous newspaper reporting, recalls being a victim himself.

Hicks, a distant cousin, was in Sue Hick's court covering one of the frequent sensational murder trials. He made the mistake of lighting up a cigarette, definitely a no-no in Judge Hicks' court.

"I knew it was taboo in Sue's presence, but I just forgot. Dan Hicks, who was reporting for the *Democrat Observer* which he owned, was thrown out of the courtroom.

Betty Byrum, a long time ad saleslady for Dan Hicks, recalled that she was a little girl when her father worked for the judge. "I got home from school one day and my mama said that 'dad was out with Sue again.'"

"For the longest time, I was mad at my daddy ... I thought he was stepping out on mama with a woman called Sue," she quipped.

Actually, it wasn't all unusual for parents to christen their sons with a girl's name when they had really hoped for a girl. Many boys in Tennessee have had to react to cruel teasing from school peers because they had the "awful" name of Lois, June, or Shirley.

The judge, it turned out, was named by his father after his mother, also named Sue, who died during childbirth.

Although Sue Hicks proved unbeatable in the many years he served as judge, he was not considered an outstanding jurist.

In fact, his one great claim to fame was being the star in Johnny Cash's hit song.

Alvin Whaley

In, April, 1985, the children of hardy mountaineer farmer, Alvin Whaley, gave their father a surprise 81st birthday party. It was out of appreciation of what their dad — who fondly described himself as one of the Greenbrier Whaleys — had done for them.

They remembered the lessons of growing up to be God-fearing, useful citizens. More than anything, his children marveled at his courage and self perseverance in taking the good with the bad. For instance, there was always the ravaging affect of the crop-eating Japanese beetles and the wrong kind of weather.

To offset this, their father would tell how his mother would take eggs to the store to buy extra food to help balance the family diet when times were hard in Greenbrier.

Life was kind in Greenbrier, even if there was barely enough money to buy clothes for the youngens. "It was a simple life, but it was a good life," Whaley said of raising in the mountains in the years before the feds drove he and many other Whaleys out to create Great Smoky Mountain National Park.

On the day of the wonderful birthday, Whaley recalled how he married his wife, the former Bessie Caughron, at Jim Allen's store in Harrisburg, 61 years before.

Whaley settled on a 69 acre farm in Maples Branch in 1924, and the hollers seemed remote from picture book Greenbrier in sprawling Sevier County.

Through the years, some of his former Greenbrier kinsmen became rich as the tourist boon hit Gatlinburg like the atom bombs falling on Hiroshima. Whaley, though, was content to work hard and sell enough burley tobacco each year to feed and clothe his family.

Alvin and Bessie wanted, more than anything, to see their children grow up to become righteous citizens … it mattered more to them than all the money-filled cash registers in Gatlinburg.

If Whaley in his twilight years had a worry, other than seeing his burley crop bring a decent price over in Newport, it was the worsening encroachment by the federal government into people's lives. What ever happened to the good old days in Greenbrier, when a man could hunt a bear or squirrel for the kitchen table — and after supper go on the front porch and pray out loud for thanksgiving?

Forced removal of his family and friends from Greenbrier and the rich Sugarlands was just the first assault by the bureaucracy. In Whaley's mind, galloping federal bureaucracy — crop quotas and the like — was making it impossible to continue the good life.

Things had changed even in Maples Branch and it wasn't all good.

"Farming looks pretty rough," he said on his 81st birthday, "and the least worry is the Japanese beetle or a hot summer's drought.

"Less than ten years ago, farmers around Maples Branch received 90 cents a pound for cattle sold in Sevierville. Now my son just told me that he can actually buy grain cheaper than corn … and at that you're turning the barest of profit.

"It's not just the Japanese beetles: the feds charge you 30 cents a pound on burley and the warehouse another dime. That's 40 cents before you even start."

"Even if you can bargain a fellow down, fertilizer is still costing every bit of $80 per ton and that's not counting the $45 for spraying the suckers and paying minimum wages for hired help," he added.

"It's so discouraging that each way you turn around, your independence is crumbling and giving away to the welfare state. In my younger days I milked 25 head of cows by hand early every morning, then to the fields and hard work for the 16-hour day.

"Now the help — if they show up at all — stands around smoking cigarettes and yapping … then expect a full day's wages.

"It's a shame that the federal government, which is supposed to be servants to the people, will give today's loafers welfare money for refusing to work."

The proud farmer who grew up in a free Greenbrier had more than made his point.

That Whaley was sick of paying excessive taxes that made government bigger and good people poorer was obviously instilled in the minds of his eight children before the fine gentleman passed on.

But his fears that the simple and good life was at the crossroads was well expressed by his son Glenn, a former county tax assessor.

"With all the high taxes brought on by so-called prosperity. I'm afraid the good days of farmers making a living by sweat and brow are gone for good," said Glenn Whaley.

Battle of Athens

The power of GI'S just victoriously back from the Great War, was probably never more evident in the United States than in the small, Southeast Tennessee city of Athens on election day in August, 1946.

Disgusted on returning from one of history's most brutal wars to find their home county still in the control of corrupt machine politics, the hardened veterans regrouped some of the esprit de corps that started a German rout at Normandy Beach.

That earth-shattering day in June, 1944 when U.S. and other allied troops landed in Normandy — and pushed the demoralized Germans on a long retreat of no return — was bantered as the "longest day."

General election day, McMinn County, Tennessee — the first Thursday of August, 1946 — ran a close second.

The election began to heat up in May at a GI rally in which reformers vowed to throw out the ruthless Democratic machine that had controlled McMinn County politics since the Great Depression. The GI's, in picking a slate of their own, found willing Republican candidates who claimed to have been cheated out of elections for years by vote-stealing politicians.

Officially, though, the horde of veterans committed to make a difference regardless of what it took, was nonpartisan. Nor did the nonpartisan GI ticket have complete support from veterans. There were some veterans who still subscribed to the old Southern Democrat philosophy that "my granpa was a good Democrat and when they pitch that last spade of dirt over my grave, they will say 'there goes another good Democrat."

Early on, the machine forces ran an advertisement in the *Athens Daily Athenian,* suggesting that the establishment had the backing of all veterans who traditionally voted Democrat.

The nonpartisan ticket countered with an ad of its own ... stoutly disclaiming any involvement with the so called GI Democrats. The ad continued in bold letters, "**The machine politicians have no interest in good government. Defeat is staring them in the face.**"

So began a long heated summer of charges and slander that served to make the county's two newspapers richer and richer.

The war of words, however, was small in comparison to the bloody violence on election day which left two deputies dead, scores injured, and decades of bitterness and distrust.

On May 17, the machine knew it was in for a fight when hundreds of boisterous veterans overfilled the armory, the largest assembly room in town. Fiery speakers railed against the Democratic administration and called for solid support for the nonpartisan ticket.

The handwriting on the wall came when Harry Johnson Jr., one of the county's most respected Democrats, confirmed that he was sick to death of dishonest leaders in his own party. He pledged to support the nonpartisan ticket to the hilt. Also pledging support for the nonpartisan ticket was Judge R.A. Davis, another respectable Democrat.

At the same time, Davis and Johnson pledged thier loyalty to the late Democrat President Franklin D. Roosevelt and the new president, Harry S. Truman.

As the GI headquarters officially opened, veterans gathered by the dozens daily, and while rehashing war stories, discussed visions for the future. They were joined by many older citizens of the community who, of course, were non-veterans, but committed to a better life for McMinn citizens.

Many citizens brought complaints of abuse from deputy sheriffs as well as gross voting fraud through the years. The reform ticket worked hard to see that both Republicans and Democrats climbed on board.

There were workshops designed to acquaint voters with voting precincts and the importance of paying poll tax in plenty of time.

At the same time, nonpartisan ticket organizers went out of the way to welcome all comers. Donations were also encouraged, and frequently, well-dressed businessmen and overall-wearing farmers handed five dollar bills and other denominations in cash to the reformers.

By the same token, the nonpartisan campaign committee kept the telephone lines busy by calling and recalling voters. Doubting Thomases who had expected the reform ticket to cave in became believers overnight. Many who had wavered jumped on the bandwagon after seeing a strong message written on a huge sign in front of party headquarters. The sign read "GI Headquarters and Phone 787."

Citizens who had long wanted change were buoyed by a tobacco chewing farmer. "I thought it was all talk, but after seeing that sign, it's not talk anymore."

After a June lull brought about by the traditional party conventions to nominate candidates, the hard-fought campaign kicked off with fervor after July 4th. The whole atmosphere was totally changed. For the first time in five years, the country was not at war. Families were united and returning soldiers found new jobs. There was a sharp increase in marriages and it marked the official beginning of the baby boom.

July in McMinn County had suddenly became the state's hottest ever election wind down month in state history. Daily newspapers from Memphis and Nashville, as well as Atlanta, Ga and New York City had converged on the city. All the time though, a new kind of fear had taken hold, as though Athens were to become victim of a new kind of warfare.

The tense atmosphere that something awful was about to happen was visioned by J.B. Collins who arrived in downtown Athens by daybreak on election day. He later recalled an ominous quiet, as though an earthquake, tornado, or other disaster were on the way to destroy the city. Everybody he saw seemed to be on edge or in a deep trance … very suspicious of whatever moved.

Collins attempted to talk with officials at the courthouse and at the jail. He found complete paranoia and even the usually talkative officials eyed Collins as though he were some kind of alien from another planet

When the polls opened, the GI election watchers were in place, as were the various precinct officers. Most were confident that, other than hard feelings over candidates and the customary tradition of passing out half-pints of bonded whiskey to influence votes, things would remain normal.

Such confidence quickly proved wishful thinking when Walter Ellis, the courthouse election judge, challenged the qualifications of a voter. Ellis was immediately arrested by watching deputies and charged with violating a federal election law.

The crowd was stunned and some protested loudly, but held their places in the voting line.

Shortly afterward, a much more serious incident occurred when Deputy Wendy Wise confronted Tom Gillespie, a Colored man who was lined up to vote at the water works.

"I told you … you were not going to vote in this precinct today," the deputy stormed at Gillespie. When Gillespie tried to ignore the lawman, Wise shot Gillespie in the side. J.C. Frye, who had left his job at ALCOA Aluminum in Blount County to come home and vote, talked Wise into putting his pistol back in to the holster.

Wise then yelled to two other deputies: "Get that nigger out of here, take him to a hospital."

The sound of the gunshot and the sight of the wounded Colored man being helped into a sheriff's car created panic in the streets.

Worse still, rumors floated to the Black Community, south of the Southern Railroad tracks, that Gillespie had died … shot in the back by Deputy Wise.

A friend of Gillespie threatened revenge on Wise. Meanwhile, unaware of trouble at the water works, GI poll watchers at the precinct in the Dixie Cafe had watched as election officials allowed numerous questionable voters to vote.

The GI's watched in frustration as the same persons returned to vote as many as three or four times. However, they could do little but object because the voters had poll tax receipts.

It was also clear that votes were being cast for dead people or persons long since moved from McMinn County.

The GI watchers had more reason to become steamed when a girl believed to be only sixteen came in to vote. She had no poll tax receipt and was not listed on the precinct list. But Deputy Minus Wilburn handed the girl a paper ballot, telling her to go ahead and vote.

This angered GI watcher Bob Hairrell who placed his hand on the ballot box and blocked her from casting a ballot. Wilburn struck Hairrell hard with his blackjack. Even though the blow knocked the veteran unconscious, Wilburn continued to hit and kick the helpless GI.

When an election observer attempted to assist Hairrell, two other deputies — Harry Hensen and "Little Man" Nichols — pulled him away. The deputies forced three other GI's into a storage room which was locked. Hairrell, beaten to a bloody pulp, was dragged over to jail.

A deputy, meanwhile, closed the precinct early, a violation of the election law. Out-of-town newspaper reporters began taking pictures of the locked precinct. That further infuriated deputies who began seizing cameras and threatening reporters.

A Memphis *Press-Scimitar* camera was seized and smashed on the sidewalk. A reporter from the *Chattanooga Times* was observed taking a picture, but managed to hide the plate before a deputy came cursing. The reporter, George Hull, tricked the deputy into taking a blank plate.

Deputies prematurely closed a second precinct at nearby Niota, but this time were overpowered by a mob of about 100 GI's. The outnumbered deputies departed, and voting continued until normal closing time. The counting showed that the GI ticket had won by a 3-1 margin, a warning to the machine that their days might be numbered.

At the Dixie Cafe, Wilburn had ordered a count in the votes. The three GI's in the back room soon realized that the balloting was being rigged. It was obvious that the old standard one to five system was in affect. Five Democrat votes would be called out to the poll recorder and one nonpartisan.

The same five to one pattern was repeated and repeated. It was clear that the Dixie Cafe precinct was being stolen by the machine.

When the polls closed, many people returned to their homes, some apparently to find safety from a still explosive situation.

A hard-core of GIs remained near the courthouse, some obviously finding courage through whiskey and moonshine. They had become fight inspired by Republican Commissioner Otto Kennedy's suggestion that they gather guns.

Hardy veteran Bill White aroused the growing crowd of GIs when he charged the deputies with being "draft-dodgers too yellow to go and fight for their country."

Kennedy's call for guns reached the ears of A.C. Owens who said he could get a supply of guns. Owens, as it turned out, had keys to the vault in the National Guard Armory. With a companion, he backed his truck against the back of the armory and began loading M-1 rifles and several boxes of ammunition in the truck.

When Owens returned to the court square he learned that other GIs had brought in their own guns. Now the GIs had an arsenal of more than thirty guns and ample ammunition.

The next few hours were remindful of Gary Cooper starring in the movie, Sgt. Alvin York. Kennedy and his brother Bull Kennedy tricked deputies into leaving the jail in groups of two to five in expectation of checking out a disturbance. The GIs would then waylay the unsuspecting deputies, disarmed them and confine the stunned deputies in a nearby garage.

More deputies in twos or threes would appear and end up on the floor of the garage with their comrades. When the deputies still in jail became aware that something was not right, they stayed put.

That was invitation for the Kennedys and their GI troopers to attack the jail. For the next thirty minutes or so, countless bullets were fired into the brick building housing the jail. What is astounding is that the GI's — most of them trained as sharp shooters bent on killing — didn't cause more casualties than happened. Nevertheless, the hundreds of bullets lodged in the brick, is testament to the fact that the last battle of the Great War happened in Athens, Tenn.

After the GI raiders succeeded in breaking into the jail, nearly twenty deputies were locked in the holding cell until they were released the next day. One of the last casualties was a deputy whose throat was cut by an assailant as he was being taken to safety by a friendly GI.

Pride of Jones Mill

The rolling store is long gone and the days of rag baloney and crackers and the warm-morning coal stove are numbered. Bernice Rainey who has operated the last of the real country stores since her husband died in 1945, was treated to a surprise 50th anniversary party in December, 1996 by a grateful community.

The celebration, amid television glare and newspaper fanfare, must have touched the souls of scores of ghosts who left their cold tobacco barns to gather around the stove and wash down baloney, cheese and crackers with big RC's and Pepsis.

Rainey's Store is certainly the last of the true country stores that represented a more caring era in the United States, most specifically the rural south.

Rainey's store is also the last breath of commercial enterprise for the tiny

community located on Highway 140 West in northwest Henry County. When Frank and Bernice Rainey bought the business during World War II, Jones Mill was a rather bustling farming community.

There were also two other combination grocery and filling stations, but the busiest activity of all went on at the large grist mill which bore the name of the community. Jones Mill which processed mill and flour from grain bought or traded from farmers, was purchased before 1920 by Taylor Holley, father of Mrs. Rainey.

Jones Mill also was blessed with a good school and Masonic lodge during the peak years of the mill operation. There was also a sawmill and garage. In the heyday of the mill when farmers waited in line for hours to unload grain, there was enough business for all.

But with the coming of automation and better transportation — Jones Mill, like the hundreds of other mills in rural Dixie — went the way of the stagecoach.

Jack Webb, a lifelong farmer, bought the mill in the 1950s and operated it until it was destroyed by fire in the early 1960s. When the mill burned, the life of Jones Mill begin to die also. For years, Rainey's Store has been the community's only business. That is only possible because of the community pride possessed by Bernice Rainey.

Bernice has tended the store and pumped gas virtually by herself since Frank passed away in 1945. During the 1940s when most of the community's young men were away defending their loved ones, Frank ran a regular rolling store which served rural households on miles of dirt and gravel roads.

As a boy growing up on my grandfather's farm nearby, I recall waiting for Frank's rolling store to stop by our house. My most precious memories was when my mother bought packages of Koolaid, which seemed to bring relief on the hot days of chopping cotton.

Rainey's store, likewise, was a break for timber cutters and farmers alike who quenched thirsts with cold dopes and finished their hard work day on healthy cuts of roll baloney and Moon pies.

Most will never again sit around the warm stove, chew the fat or entertain into night with checker games, while seated on nail kegs.

But the memory of the departed ... the greats with names like Jones, Paschall, Fletcher and Holley will in spirit, hold their places around the warm fire as long as the old store remains.

A few of the gems remain and most joined Mrs. Rainey at her proudest day in late 1996.

Folks like Harold and Wade Holley, Clarence Paschall and James Boyd Harding.

Ever the gracious lady, Bernice has vowed to keep the store open until she is able no longer to tote in a bucket of coal or pump gas for a wayward traveler.

Then there are the younger generations ... they cry out that the circle not be unbroken. Folks like Joe Taylor Rainey, her son and sister-in-law, Peggy Holley.

Farmers like Dan Paschall, Ronnie Bell and Steve Parrish — the younger generations remember how their elders loved the country store. And there is Kyle Veazey going on 14 ... that boy has a lot of get up and go and the will to carry on the tradition.

Must the circle be unbroken?

Dolly Loved the Mountain Boy
With the Sexy Nose Holes

H ad not Dolly Parton found in stant success in country music and Hollywood, she probably would have married her high school beau with the sexy noseholes. And likely they'd settled down in Boogertown ... raising a passel of children.

Donnie Trotter, in an interview for an article I wrote in June, 1986 for the *Mountain Press,* was courting Dolly real seriously in 1963 and 1964 when they were classmates at Sevier County High School in Sevierville.

Letters and photographs they shared showed, indeed, that their romance was just the tonic that resulted in teen lovers getting married and staying in their raisings, especially if both were poor folks in the mountains.

They both shared the typical mountain birthright of knowing what it was to eat dried peas for breakfast, and drink enough water at dinner so the peas would swell up and burst for supper.

During their latter high school years, the steady sweethearts drove around the hollers in the Boogertown and Catons Chapel hollers in Donnie's old car. Always low on gas, Trotter kept a few strands of baling wire for an emergency.

Indications that the romance was one of passion came from a letter Dolly penned Trotter in his 1964 high school yearbook. Reminding her old flame of their "regular routine," Dolly wrote, "Don't forget the time you almost tore the gallus buckle off my overhauls?"

Indeed — after 22 years which found the teen lovers in two different worlds — Donnie hadn't forgotten their "regular routine."

"We'd drive around through the night, even though we seldom had money for movies. We'd drink Cokes and drive some more. Finally we'd stop somewhere in the country so she could relieve herself of the Cokes.

"Boy … it's a good thing for her that the taillights of my old car couldn't see or take pictures … although, ha-ha, the side mirror and brake lights worked pretty well," mused Trotter.

As the moonlight sparkled on Dolly's red, juicy lips and the combination of her "come get me" look, Trotter thought about scoring.

"Her tempting look and pretty wide eyes sure did something to a lovesick mountain boy. I'd say to myself … 'self, now's the time to really make your move.'

"That's when she'd start telling me about how handsome and beautiful and sexy my nose holes were."

Teasing or not, by Dolly's own admission, Trotter was her number one lover in those years. In fact, that was the exact message she penned on her first record, "I Wasted My Tears," which she gave to Trotter, along with two spicy imprints of her red lipstick kisses on the record cover.

The Day a Little Girl's Ghost Returned
to Haunt Cottage Grove

E ven in the 1880s, when Cottage Grove had at least three saloons, it's not likely that the small, Northwest Henry County town was touched with more imagination than the day the hundred-year-old dead girl returned.

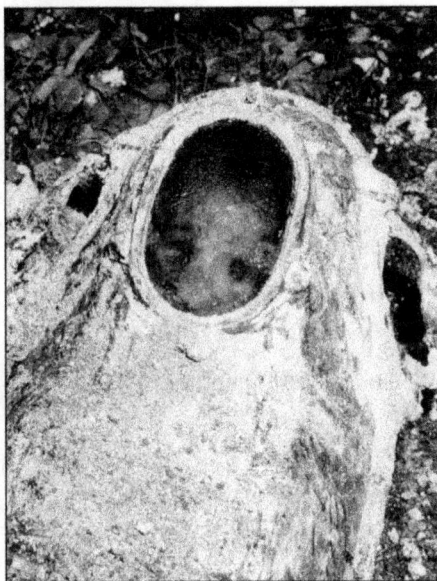

You might say that Cottage Grove had its day but blew it. Settled in the 1840s, the village once was a busy agricultural community, having a grist mill, tobacco warehouse, broom factory, tannery, cotton gin, and other small industries.

It was more than your usual frontier one-horse town in that it had several grocery and dry goods stores, jewelry, hotel, theater, garages and blacksmith shops. Even through the World War II years, the town had at least four general stores which attracted much trade from area counties.

Then something happened that turned the community from the county's second largest city to a near ghost town. Many people blamed it on overzealous 1880s elders who rejected an offer by a railroad baron to run tracks through the town. One widely discussed excuse was that the shrill sound of railroad steam whistles would disrupt the peaceful calm of the community, even interfere with the hens laying their eggs.

Others think that once a wave of temperance set in, which resulted in the ban on saloons, the town became too entrenched in Puritan ways for its own good.

Whatever the reason, Cottage Grove's only present claim to fame is having the dubious distinction of being Tennessee's smallest incorporated town. This was publicized in 1996 by the *Wall Street Journal* and picked up by other news outlets across the nation.

Even the *Wall Street Journal* scoop could not hold a light to a morning in the early 1960s when a well-preserved corpse of a small child erupted suddenly from the ground, following hours of hard rainfall.

Certainly, Joy Call and Camille Rainey had no thoughts of starting a national sensation as they leisurely strolled down Church Street to visit a high school classmate.

The two close friends were younger generations of very prominent families which had provided the leadership that helped the town prosper in the post Civil War era.

Camille whose father, J.T. Rainey, headed the successful Cottage Grove Bank & Trust Company, is now deceased. Miss Call has served as a gifted teacher and principal in the Paris Special School District.

Joy isn't sure who saw the glass-enclosed metal casket of the little girl's body first. But she is sure that both teens simultaneously let out bloodcurdling screams, alerting neighbors that something wasn't just right in Cottage Grove on that bright spring day.

The casket had found its way to sunlight after steady erosion on a slope at the edge of what had been a family burial ground. The girl was remarkably preserved, appearing very much a living doll, with dark black hair and nose surprisingly intact.

Within a few hours, television and newspaper reporters from distant cities had opened road maps to pinpoint Cottage Grove. By nightfall, an army of reporters and photographers had descended on the town.

Articles appeared in such newspapers as the Memphis *Commercial Appeal* and Louisville *Courier-Journal.* Many inhabitants of Cottage Grove glued themselves to the television that night to see if they had been caught by the scan of the TV cameras.

At long last, Cottage Grove was on the map ... if for odds bordering on about a million to one.

The corpse of the girl — believed to have died about the time of the War for Southern Independence — was reburied by a Paris funeral home at an undisclosed burial site.

For months, the finding of the long deceased girl, whose surname was revealed as Todd, was the supper table topic of conversation throughout Cottage Grove and its large rural community side. Even now, Miss Call is frequently contacted by newspapers for background information, as well as people from other states who have roots in the area.

At the time the Todd girl's corpse was uncovered, I was teaching in Anniston, Alabama. Having grown up on a farm three miles north of Cottage Grove and attending its schools, I naturally was interested when my mother sent me newspaper clippings of the incident.

That first hand imagination, though, was nothing compared with the excitement when I learned several years afterward that the Todd girl is my ancestor.

The Todd girl was an aunt of Mary Hunt Dumas, my grandmother. And now, out of curiosity, I'd like to know the location of the Todd girl's new burial site.

I'd like to leave flowers on special occasions, like on Jefferson Davis' birthday. After all, Davis likely was her only president ... if her life took place when the South was a separate nation.

Z. Buda, Fiery Mayor of Morristown, Brings Down Governor

When, in 1970, scholarly Memphis dentist Winfield Dunn was elected Tennessee's first Republican governor in 50 years, it sent shock waves through the Democratic party.

Dunn might be governor today had he not messed with a feisty Morristown mayor named Z. Buda.

Over Buda's protests the Dunn administration wanted to build one of its pet regional prisons in Morristown, county seat of the Northeast Tennessee county of Hamblen.

The state did complete the multimillion dollar project, although it was clear that a majority of Morristown residents were in opposition.

Early one morning, as workers headed to the project site, they found their progress blocked by a steamed Mayor Buda, leading an army of upset citizens.

The building was too far completed and the contract too cemented, but that incident and further verbal assaults from the mayor convinced Dunn and the state Corrections System not to use the facility as a prison.

Dunn's rather foolhardy attempt to force the prison on a community which was near united in opposition would haunt him 14 years later when the tooth doctor tried a political comeback.

Feeling pretty confident that traditionally strong Republican Northeast Tennessee would return him to the governor's office over formidable opponent Ned Ray McWherter, Dunn looked up Buda at Z's outlet mall empire in Pigeon Forge.

Dunn recalled that Buda, who had since retired from politics, had given him money and votes when he scored an upset victory in November, 1969.

To give credit where due, Dunn was an impressive campaigner. His mild-mannered ways and sincerity had much to do with his win over Democrat John Jay Hooker.

And what the heck? He might have ruffled Buda over the Morristown prison issue, but after all, Z. Buda was known as a staunch Republican.

"I want you to help me," said Dunn as he reached for Buda's hand on a hot September morning.

"I'll help you? I'll help beat you," fired back Buda. Those who heard the exchange compared Dunn with a whimpered pup ... a whimpered, beaten pup.

The healthy campaign donation that Winfield Dunn hoped to pocket from Buda that morning went instead in the pocket of House Speaker McWherter.

McWherter went on to become the first Democrat ever to win Hamblen County and the normally Republican First District stronghold.

Dunn would have at least come closer and not been embarrassed in his big support base had he taken a few minutes to pay closer scrutiny to that crusty mayor who led the rebellion against the prison at Morristown.

If so, he might have made use of Buda's fighting instinct. Whether in politics or business, Z was a real winner.

A populist and proven friend of the working folks ... even his strong ties as a University of Alabama football supporter never hurt his vote getting ability in crazed University of Tennessee Big Orange country.

Blessed with uncanny business foresight, Buda was one of the first vision-aries to see that the mostly corn and tobacco fields that landscaped sleepy Pigeon Forge would soon give way to hotels and restaurants in the tourist boom that hit Gatlinburg.

Even as he continued to win the mayoral election in Morristown, Buda invested in Pigeon Forge real estate, buying one of the area's more popular restaurants in the process.

Later he brought in the attraction, Mountain Ocean — a kind of artificial roaring inland sea that delighted kids and grown-up alike. Buda was the first to introduce Grand Ole Opry style music to the area, featuring Bonnie Lou and Buster.

He closed his Mountain Ocean when he saw that tourists from a few miles away to the Pacific Coast were about to go crazy over outlet stores. He built the first outlet mall in the resort town, sold it for a profit, built another, and suddenly had more competition than a fast food restaurant.

Buda never tried to run for political office in Pigeon Forge. He realized that an outsider is at a disadvantage in a community where natives claim so many kin folks.

But he hasn't dodged the first confrontation from city hall. Several years ago the city council, composed mainly of hotel owners, pushed through a controversial sign ordinance, setting rigid restrictions on business advertising.

For years, the Z Buda Coliseum was recognized readily by tourists because of an old bus out front, advertising Bonnie Lou and Buster. After the ordinance passed, Buda received a summons to the city judge's chamber to answer why his bus shouldn't be removed.

When Buda barged into the chambers with excited and glaring eyes remindful of Confederate General Nathan Bedford Forrest at Parkers Cross Roads, all present knew there would be a hot time in the old town.

Buda's answer was one that the city officials obviously hadn't prepared for: Silver Dollar City — which still owns Dollywood, despite the myth — had years before brought in two silver rail dining cars that once rolled on Southern Railroad tracks through the South.

Silver Dollar City served tourists fancy meals as in the passenger train heyday. But the big draw for the German Missouri family that owns Silver Dollar City (and Dollywood), was that it pointed the way to the amusement park, free advertising that can't be bought.

"I'll move my bus when I see Silver Dollar City pulling their dining cars down the parkway toward Knoxville.

End of the confrontation.

Bumpus Mills

They used to rob the bank with a regularity that matched the change of seasons, but ninety-five year old Emma Smith believes that the U.S. Army was the real culprit that reduced Bumpus Mills from a thriving and promising town to a wide place in the road.

She remembers the good old days when farmers from two counties lined the roads while bringing their wheat to the only flour processing mill in Stewart County.

"But Fort Campbell came to Clarksville and pretty soon the government took over just about all the good farm land we had," the lady deplored.

Mrs. Smith, a widow who still lives in the family homeplace on a hill overlooking the dying town in southern Stewart County, is herself a matriarch of the Bumpus family which came to Middle Tennessee in the early 1900s.

Located on Highway 120 about ten miles southeast of Dover, the seat of Stewart County, Bumpus Mills once had several general stores, a blacksmith, hardware stores, and assorted businesses. Like other viable rural towns across the South following the War for Southern Independence, Bumpus Mills provided all that farmers would need.

"We didn't need Clarksville, Paris, or some of the bigger shopping cities. We had all we needed to get us by, sold right here in Bumpus Mills. On Saturdays and the days before Christmas, our stores were plumb full and people by the dozens walked to and fro ... from store to store," recalled Mrs. Smith,

But every town is kept together by some type of industry which not only supplies jobs, but the base industry that attracts buyers 10 to 30 miles away, it's the lifeblood of a community. In this case it was Bumpus Grain Mill, the drawing point which brought farmers and their families to exchange wheat for fresh flour and to browse around the stores while waiting.

However, with the decline of the mill, the town's business took a nose dive.

Not only were stores forced into bankruptcy, but the high school closed, and in more recent years the grade school was also consolidated with other community schools.

"We was doing just fine and we lived happily with our own kind of people until Fort Campbell took all the good wheat land from us," repeated Mrs. Smith.

Even after the government began seizing farming land in Montgomery and Stewart counties to expand Fort Campbell — home of the 101st Airborne — Bumpus Mills remained in the news. However, the news wasn't the kind that towns love to hear. For some reason, the one bank in Bumpus Mills became a favorite target for armed robbers. The bank was robbed so often, it became a joke from Nashville to the Kentucky border, north of Paris, Tenn.

The low point came when the bank was held up by a one-legged man who escaped with the aid of a crutch.

Fortunately, the one-legged man was soon caught, but others apparently kept their ill-gotten loot for life.

Ironically, long before the town had a bank of its own, Bumpus Mills citizens still had a difficult time banking their savings. Mrs. Smith recalls in the late 1920s when the president of a bank in Dover — a Mr. Peck — came to Bumpus Mills and talked several people into depositing their money at his bank.

"My husband was Elfry Smith and he was one of the folks Mr. Peck talked

into putting all his money in his bank. The very next year the bank went busted in the Depression. Elfry lost $1,500 … all he had, and on today's level that was the same as $100,000.

"My husband got real mad and I remember he said: 'That Peck old devil, he knew the bank would go busted all along.'"

Mrs. Smith — one of Stewart County's most interesting persons — was born and raised in a holler not far from Dover, called Tobacco Fork. She said the community got its name because tobacco farmers brought their tobacco there to be stacked, before loaded on a barge and hauled down the Cumberland River to markets in Clarksville.

The youngest of twelve children, she was the daughter of Desmond Hargis. Family genealogy has her great grandfather, Andrew Jackson "Ole Jack" Bumpus, loading his family in covered wagons in North Carolina in the early 1840s, bound for Tennessee to find virgin farm land.

The Bumpus family settled briefly in White County — halfway between Knoxville and Nashville — before deciding on going further west. After reaching Stewart County, and unwilling to ford the Tennessee River again, the family made their new home in the area later called Tobacco Fork.

Years later, Desmond Hargis, who was her father, married into the Bumpus family. Although Mrs. Smith was the youngest of the children — and the only survivor — she remembers well the dangers of the frontier life.

With little law for protection, the early settlers in the area had to often arm themselves to protect their loved ones from highwaymen who thought nothing of killing for their ill-gotten gain.

"My grandfather, Lionel Desmond, was a justice of the peace and when the court met at Dover he'd come riding in by horse and buggy and a rifle laying across his lap," recalled Mrs. Smith.

The high wooded hills and dense hollers in Stewart County made it a haven for moonshiners. That was reason enough for thinking men to arm themselves when traveling. It wasn't that the moonshiners — most of them decent poor people making a living — wanted to bring harm to anyone. They just didn't want anyone to discover their illegal stills.

Mrs. Smith said that although moonshine could cause a person to become violent and threaten his family, it still had a good point. "Just about all the farmers and city folks, too, kept a little moonshine. A man never knew when he needed a little sip to settle his nerves, but it also was used to kill a bad cold."

Indeed, rural people in the South found that a touch of whiskey, sugar and lemon, was effective in relieving the croup and bad colds in children as well as grown-ups.

Mrs. Smith recalls that her stern mother, Mary Elizabeth Shelton Hargis, was successful in teaching her twelve children to walk the walk and talk the talk. "My mother believed in strict discipline and when one of us children broke her rules, woe be us.

"She had strong principles and thought it was a sin for girls and ladies to straddle a saddle while riding a horse. I wasn't all that crazy by riding on a sidesaddle, so I guess I walked to church and school more than I rode a horse or buggy," she quipped.

Emma was so opposed to riding sidesaddle, she said, that she usually walked about a mile-and a-half to Glendale Institute, a 1-to-12 grade public school just outside Bumpus Mills. "Not only do I remember walking hundreds of miles before I graduated, but I also remember my first grade teacher. She was Annie Walker and I learned a lot from her," she asserted.

"My mother believed, simply, that if you were born for hell that's where you'd go. But if you were born for Heaven, you'd end up there. She did her best to see that all her children were destined for Heaven."

She remembers that her mother's excellent cooking served as a excuse for the preacher to pay the family a visit as well as drummers who came to Bumpus Mills on steamboats to peddle their goods.

She was there once when a Jewish ginseng exporter from Clarksville called on the family. "Because he was Jew, he said he couldn't eat pork except under certain conditions.

"But mother would put pork, mutton, and a lot of vegetables on his plate. She'd say … 'there's the pork and I took the pains of poaching you an egg. You can suit yourself to arrange it any way you see fit.'

"That old Jew always seemed to find some excuse, because the pork didn't last any longer than the vegetables," she chuckled.

Mrs. Smith recalls that travel was seldom easy, particularly on one particular creek where water was frequently too high for horses and buggies to ford the stream.

"The first real progress I knew was when the county built an iron bridge across the creek in 1912. But in 1928 I was scared to death when a big tornado came across our land and blowed the bridge away,"

Mrs. Smith recalls when members of the Hargis family operated the old Herndon Hotel at Bumpus Mills during horse and buggy days. "One of my brothers ran the hotel and traveling people was always lined up, hoping to get a room early in the evening."

Later, one of Mrs. Smith's sisters, who had married Wayne Clark, managed the inn.

The Clarks' daughter, Virginia Clark — a retired school teacher — still lives in the handsome, big, two-story white frame house where she was born. The house sits on a grassy hill, a stone's throw from where Emma lives.

The situation couldn't be more ideal for Emma, who is visited daily by her niece. Nor could it be for Virginia who brings food to her aunt and listens in awe as Emma tells her another chapter about the interesting first family of Bumpus Mills.

Harold Chance Sure Outfoxed 'Em

In the early 1980s, a lot of mountain folks made light of the fact that a Sevierville newspaper's annual poll of Sevier County's People Movers and Shakers generally listed the same citizens. I recall one mountaineer referring to the selections as "millionaires hall of fame."

At the time, I was editor and publisher of a Pigeon Forge weekly I had co-founded called the *Smoky Mountain Star*. One morning I walked into Johnson's restaurant, where the usual bunch came to drink coffee early in the morning and try to solve the world's problems.

Many of them, in fact, could have been classed millionaires too ... the good old boys had done quite well — given the sudden prosperity dumped in their laps. But they didn't want to be lumped in the same category with the blue bloods in Sevierville who were raised on a silver spoon.

One of them suggested that since I ran the *Star* — and was their kind of people — that I was duty bound to poll a separate list of movers and shakers. One that appealed to the working man, the bear hunter, the hard beer drinker, and what few Democrats they allowed to live in Sevier County. I thought about it as I was making my daily news beats between Sevierville and Gatlinburg ... when I happened to see Harold Chance come out of a market with a six pack. Presto! I had found the man to head the 'poor boys' Movers and Shakers.

Not there's not much you can do that Harold hadn't already done. Once he was playing poker with some hard beer drinkers out of Cocke County. Chance was having unbelievablly good luck, as if it were taking his surname seriously.

Harold was about ready to cash in on his easily inherited loot, when one of the sore losers pushed his chair from the table and stomped out in the dark of night.

Then, the man returned to the game and there was something definitely hissing from the pocket of his trench coat. It was a rattlesnake, obviously all the madder that his nap had been interupted.

The sore loser — who they say held the snake's slivering head as if he had worshiped in one of those Holyiness churches — aimed squarely at the poker game. They gave the room to the snake man — cards, table, money and all.

Believe it or not — what went on at the poker table — was merely typical in the life of Harold Chance. Always a candidate for constable, he once was down in the dumps after losing the election 163-7.

Harold said he had learned one thing from that first election ... "With no more friends than that, I decided I better start toting a gun fast"

It can be said that Chance was never a quitter, and in the next election for constable, Harold had handed out enough half-pints of rot gut to his friends in Frog Alley to beat his opposition handily.

Harold was used to carrying a gun, especially when he ventured around the hills and stills over in Cocke County. Being constable meant it was now legal.

His friends, and those who were not friendly, swore on a Bible that Chance had never arrested a soul during his years as lawman. And there were plenty in his district who needed arrested.

He did try one time. Sevier County — being a mountainous county where few slaves existed — didn't have a large colored population. In fact, when Chance was robbed at the poker game, the census listed no more than 25 black citizens in the entire county.

For some reason, Chance decided to arrest one of them. He was making steady progress toward the jail when the man grabbed Harold's pistol and shot him in the foot. Chance is still the only constable in the East Tennessee mountains who never made an arrest.

But that wasn't the reason why I picked him to head the *Star*'s list of top movers and shakers. Despite the progress that had made Gatlinburg the big tourist attraction of Dixie, Sevierville was a totally dry town. It seemed that the mayor and council wanted to keep it that way and it happened that the top mover and shaker picked in the poll by the other paper was the mayor.

Harold and some of his friends had been rebuffed by the council in their efforts to livened the place up. Now Harold could be called a lot of things in his life time, and indeed he was called a lot of things. But Chance was no dummy ... nobody ever said "he just got off the cabbage truck yesterday."

Chance happened to own a house and maybe three acres of land that bordered city limits. The city had annexed in the county up to Harold's property — maybe they didn't want Chance in the city. Mayor Clifford Davis, the previous mayor, had led a drive to build a new city park which bordered Chance's property.

It was a nice park, too, plenty of softball and little league baseball fields.

Chance decided one morning that since the county allowed the sale of beer, he'd apply for a license. He was so sure of his chances that he built a shack right on the city property line.

Naturally the mayor and council put up a howl, but the county beer board said that Harold had abided by the rules. Chance was legally selling beer right on the city boundary and there wasn't a thing the city could do about it.

That is, except to buy him out. After Harold spent a few months aggravating the mayor and council, he sent word he would sell his property to the city ... but not a bit cheap.

The council — which had become a laughing stock because of Harold's needling ways — was glad to pay a big price to close Harold's beer joint.

And that's why Harold was selected top dog on the *Star*'s first and last Movers and Shakers.

Cooking On a Wood Stove
& Traipsing to a Privy

T he wonders of push-button electric lights and indoor plumbing just don't impress Hinda Green Thompson. You might say she inherited her independence from her mother, Allie Chilcutt Green, who in 1950 boycotted a utility system's offer to finally bring rural electricity to the Buchanan community in northeast Henry County.

The development of Kentucky Lake which touches the largest acres of shorelines in the nation, vastly changed the environment and culture of the once heavy cotton growing piedmont forever. But it didn't change Hinda Thompson.

She continues to live in the modest two-story white frame house on a scenic knoll overlooking the lake. Neighbors who reside in $500,000 to $800,000 brick homes think Hinda is out of place.

What would those neighbors know? Many hail from the North and have no feeling at all of how Buchanan natives survived, planting cotton and tobacco the old-fashioned way, killing hogs and cooking good Southern meals on wood range stoves and leaving a warm fire on freezing nights to go to the outdoor privy. What do those Yankees know about what it takes to make a Southern rebel happy?

Her nearest neighbor, by the way, is country music star Hank Williams, Jr.

Despite Hank's wealth and fame, he knows well the hard times his famous daddy had growing up on a sharecropper farm in rural South Alabama during the Great Depression.

As for Hinda, she continues to read by a coaloil lamp and cook her meals over the same wood range that was her mother's. For cooking and washing clothes, she pulls buckets of water from a cistern just as she did while a young girl attending Buchanan School.

She often drinks the cistern water just as all hard working farming families did, until rural electrification took away much of the simple life. Hinda prefers — and who can fault her — to take a bucket down the steep hill to the spring and depend on that for drinking water. After all, her ancestors of earlier generations kept a worn patch to the spring.

As for satellite television, modern vacuum cleaners, mixers, and refrigeration, the proud lady — about 68 — could care less. Hinda reflects entertainment and education from reading several books a week. On that score handed down from our rural ancestors, children today are set back terribly.

She may not have a vacuum cleaner or bright lights. But I defy you to find a cleaner house in West Tennessee. The same is true for the outside, as Hinda's colorful flowers and blooming plant life compliments her dedication to neatness.

Health? The biggest sham in the post World War II era is the Washington D.C. bureaucrat who, in his warped mind, thinks that rural Southerners are inferior because they eat fatty pork not inspected by other bureaucrats and keep canned jars of sausage and vegetables in damp well houses.

It's for sure, Winn Dixie and Jim Adams IGA don't get rich off Hinda and other self-sufficient people like her. Her grandparents survived on blackstrap sorghum molasses and salt-cured ham from the smoke house.

For bad colds, she avoids $60 physician office calls and takes a few spoons of coaloil and sugar. That remedy relieved cold symptoms for her parents and grandparents. Anyway, medical science in all its awesome progress still hasn't found a cure for croup and bad colds.

Actually, she prefers to live mainly on dry foods, which also lessens her dependency for stocking ice in the old-fashioned ice box to preserve meats and other food.

Just as her grandfathers had to, Hinda keeps warm on the coldest of nights by crowding the large living room fire place. When it gets to 15 below zero, as it occasionally does, to the chagrin of Yankee imports, Hinda heats up the wood range stove too.

Despite her old-fashioned preference, old friends of the family, like Rubye Lee Housden Harris, often stop by to chat. A look back at the years of coaloil lamps, outhouses, and cisterns restores cherished memories of their childhood.

Hank Jr., when he interrupts his busy tour for a few days fishing on the lake, has stopped by to chat also.

It's been said that today's spoiled generations of baby boomers and other children could not bear the thought of sleeping without an air conditioner or not being able to see pro football on television.

The brats might be better served to take a cue from Hinda Thompson and sleep by an open window and read a good book.

Jack's Amazing Pool Hall

There's a pool room in Paris with a history dating back sixty years. There's a legend that Minnesota Fats once shot billiards there, not to mention the awesome pool sharks that rode into town from Chicago or Little Rock to win a pretty penny at Jack's Southern famous Pool Room.

In sheer redneck idol worship though, Fats and the road sharks couldn't hold a cueball to home town heroes of the past like Monk Foust, Tommy Brown, Jimmy Seawright, Frog Dotson or Elliott Moody.

Those days of the cool shooting roadmen riding into town like Shane to take on the best have gone the way of the steam propelled passenger train. Now and then somebody — maybe from as far as Cairo, Illinois — will try to hustle a little easy money in pool halls down in Dixie.

At Jack's they'll try and sic him on Larry Blackburn, the kingpin of Paris pool shooters. Now and in a great while, Larry will meet his match. But down here, he's still kingpin. Other fair-to-midlin shooters who hang their hats in Jack's include Otis "The Professor" Ferguson, Dale Brown, Kenneth Castleman and Randy Mohon.

The business was founded during the Great Depression by Dick and Jack Brockwell and known as Brockwell Brothers until the end of the Great War when the brothers went their separate ways.

Dick opened up a pool hall about two blocks north of the courthouse and Jack about two blocks east of the courthouse, if that signifies an omen of some sort.

At the time the city had six pool halls downtown: one in West Paris, formerly a busy rail passenger-freight terminal on the L & N, and at least one in the outskirts of town.

Other pool rooms included City Billiards, owned by Joe Seawright, which was next door to old City Hall, and the Dixie Pool Room. Seawright's City Billiards is where Monk usually hung his cue stick and that deserves some press. Foust was one of the familiar characters that every town in Dixie used to have.

They stand out for both the outlandish and the innocent things they have done. One of Monk's greatest claims to the billiard hall of fame — other than running the tables on unsuspecting sharks now and then — was an uncanny ability to down a gooseneck bottle of Griesedieck Brothers beer in one sensational gulp.

Each day before dinner, Joe would walk out the back door and down the alley to deposit the up-to-date receipts in Commercial Bank. He'd leave Monk behind the bar to wait on customers. The second Monk saw Joe's back exiting the door, he'd open the cooler, lower his head as though he was fooling those other rednecks, and down the cold Griesey before you could utter "Jack Robinson."

They say that ole Monk downed over three beers before Joe had returned from the bank. Monk wasn't fooling ole Seawright one iota. One time Joe went out the back door and immediately came back in, just as Monk was chaffing another beer.

Monk looked at Joe and said ... damnit Joe, that ain't fair. Joe just chuckled and resumed his walk toward the bank, leaving a couple more Griesediecks at the mercy of Monk Foust.

Before Jack passed away several years ago, he sold the business to Steve Cannon, who had by then bought half-interest in the pool room.

Under Cannon, the landmark pool room has continued to thrive, although the six pool tables aren't near as busy as in the golden years of billiard halls.

One of the biggest changes was in admitting women, which, until the late 1960s at least, was considered taboo. Go back to the Depression years, most good mothers didn't allow their young daughters to even walk past pool halls. Women who did so were considered ladies of the evening or in modern lingo, a simple whore.

Cannon enjoys a pretty profitable trade from women customers, including many well-dressed in business garb who stop by to eat a snack that includes Jack's famous hamburgers and S.O.S.

Occasionally, a road woman will walk in to show the boys her pool talents, while other gals frequent by in short shorts to show off their God-given wares.

As from the beginning, upper class, richer men will drop by, like lawyers Dick Dunlap, Gary Swayne and Jim Fields. Dr. David Travis, a local dentist, is a frequent fan of Jacks, as are bank presidents David Flowers and Jack Veazey.

They, like personable Whitlock Mayor Junior Ross and Ronnie Lampkins, remain longtime steady customers. Charlie Reddin and caterer Donald Davenport like to drop in after a hard day's work. Sometimes, they pick up clients for their own enterprises.

Doug Davis who spends winters in the warmer climate of South Texas, is usually in Jack's during summer months, if he's not fishing on Kentucky Lake.

Politicians seeking votes stream into the pool hall before election time, and in a close race that could be crucial, especially if they buy the house a round.

U.S. Senator Fred Thompson came into Jack's the first campaign visit he paid Paris in 1994. Fred, also a movie actor, never fails to stop in for a cool Bud when he's in town.

Home town fellows like Randy Patrick and Mark and Bart Herbison, who made it big in Nashville, help exemplify the good memories that former Parisians hold for Jack's Pool Room. When the old boys return home to visit, they stampede to Jacks.

Of course it would not be appropriate if I failed to mention Dwight "Big D" Milton who has been a faithful employee at Jack's for years. Big D likes to keep the customers entertained with his tall tales about being a star quarterback for LSU. Now and then some poor soul will drift by and actually believe him.

Then there's Hawk Miller who stops by at the top of the morning to read the daily newspapers. Hawk's a legend in his own time.

And there's the redneck's favorite, ole Bruce. Bruce commutes from McKenzie everyday because he's so crazy about Jack's atmosphere.

I guess if the truth were known, I relate back a long time in the history of Jack's. Country boys like R.G. Davemport, Buddy Parrish, Jerry Callicott, and I used to wait a long time for a table at Jack's when we came to town on a Saturday night.

And what greater memory can a Southern rebel redneck have than for the old Western Union ticker tape in Jack's and City Billiards which kept you abreast of big league baseball, better than TV, back before the era of the crybaby million dollar players who aren't even worth shooting.

John Hunt Finds His Roots at Last

J ohn C. Hunt long ago found a successful life in Paris, France. An official in French government and president of agricultural-related industries in Kansas City, Mo., he was in his early sixties before learning that his roots were in another Paris, far across the ocean in Tennessee.

In the interval, Hunt spent thousands of dollars on a genealogical trace which even his experienced Tennessee genealogist was skeptical about.

That's because Hunt had virtually no information about who he was. All he had was a sheet of paper with six names. It had been many years since his paternal grandmother gave him that scrap of paper with the mysterious names.

Hunt was still a boy when his grandmother gave him the six names scribbled on the back of a bank note in Muskogee, Okla., his birthplace. For a few years he was puzzled about the world shaking emphasis his grandmother seemed to have placed on the paper,

"Someday, you'll know who you are."

But as Hunt neared manhood, went off to college, and later joined the Marines at the outbreak of the Great War, the piece of paper was among the least of his concerns.

About ten years ago, Hunt was looking through old documents left by his paternal grandparents when the long-forgotten little piece of paper fell loose.

For the first time, he carefully studied the names: John Crockett, David Crockett, John Wesley Crockett, Elizabeth Crockett Tharpe, Henry Clinton Hunt, Mead Kinghorn Hunt.

Suddenly the mere names scribbled so long ago by his grandmother seemed to take on meaning akin to the moving of a whole mountain. Could Henry Hunt be his father? Like everybody the world over, he was fascinated with the folk legend, David Crockett. Was it possible?

It was then that Hunt began a full scale effort to find his identity by hiring Brenda Johnson, a noted genealogist in Memphis. But it wasn't until Ms. Johnson — trying to decipher the Tharpe connection — contacted Billie Dumas in Paris, that she was confident the search was over.

Mrs. Dumas, the widow of Howard Dumas, a former farmer, politician, and automobile dealer, and my mother, is a great-great-granddaughter of Colonel William A. Tharpe, a War of 1812 veteran and one of Tennessee's largest land and slave owners before the War for Southern Independence.

The telephone call from Memphis to Paris was to be Hunt's first significant break in his lifelong search to find his roots. Mrs. Dumas' late mother-in-law, it turned out, was Mary Hunt, who also was John's great aunt.

Mrs. Dumas' great aunt, Mary Tharpe, married John C. Hunt, which means that she and John Hunt of Paris, France are double second cousins.

Hunt said learning that he was a fourth great-grandson of David Crockett was worth the decades of pain of searching for his identity. "Who would have known fifty years ago that I would be in Henry County — the origin of my roots — and be staring down at the grave of David Crockett's son, John Wesley?"

Hunt's three-day visit to Henry County included visiting old graveyards, some located in desolate woods which he walked difficult terrain and climbed rusty barbed-wire fences to reach.

The humidity was frightfully hot the day that Hunt, Mrs. Dumas, and I hiked through a wheat field in the Northwest part of the county to Powell Cemetery.

The graveyard was fairly big, but the three visitors found many tombstones broken or overturned because of dense brush and other growth. Several of Hunt's and my ancestors are buried there. In winter months following heavy rains, it's impossible even for horses to get across the marshy field leading up to the knoll that is Powell Cemetery.

At least one older member of the Hunt family, who was supposed to have been buried at Powell, was buried instead at Walker Cemetery. Pall bearers simply could not carry the coffin in the flooded area.

Hunt immediately found the graves of ancestors he didn't know existed. He was about to leave, very disappointed about not finding his great-great-grandfather's grave, when one of us tripped over a fallen marker that was half buried and covered with leaves. It was his great-great-grandfather's, John Butler Hunt.

Hunt had similar luck finding relatives on his mother's side of the family too. At Crutchfield Cemetery in Paris — which also required a lengthy, though easier, walk — he saw the grave of another great-great-grandfather, Blake Crutchfield. Crutchfield, who built the first grist mill in the county, also was a large landowner. One of his loyal slaves, who had requested to be buried at the foot of his former master, was given that wish.

Crutchfield is also my great-great-grandfather.

Hunt, elated, also saw a tall monument honoring another of his illustrious ancestors, Colonel William A. Tharpe, his third great-grandfather, at Tharpe Cemetery in East Paris.

While Hunt continues to communicate frequently with Mrs. Dumas and other members of the Hunt family, such as Carolyn Ann Akers, he hasn't had an occasion to return to his roots, which he has vowed to do.

The brief visit in 1993 was spent largely in graveyards or consumed in courthouse and library research. He just didn't have that much time to visit relatives.

But thanks to that little piece of scrap paper and the six names, he learned about a lot of kin folks.

Palestine's Lady Farmer

She may not be the best farmer in the world, but few doubt that the personable blonde who specializes in grooming feeder pigs and quality dairy cows in Palestine is Tennessee's prettiest one.

Going on thirty and divorced, Leah Kloppenstein could be a socialite in most any of the posh country clubs for miles around. College educated and skilled in computer software, the lady could land a comfortable job in high tech and quickly climb the ladder of success.

But Leah spends lots of nights as a midwife and helps one of her cows deliver a newborn calf.

Her exercise comes not from jogging through a residential neighborhood, but from repairing fences, bailing hay and dehorning cattle. She's a levelheaded administrator, who carefully weighs decisions before investing in more livestock and new equipment.

Plenty of women are seen pushing a lawn mower, but you'd more likely see Leah scraping manure from the barn yard or cutting hay.

She plans for a more profitable future by renting unused land to neighboring farmers.

She's a native rural Ohio girl — who was raised in a staunchly rebel West Tennessee county that proudly sent sons to kill Yankee invaders from Ohio 136 years ago. Though she was only four when her dad chose to move South, she remembers well the basic values of the people who tilled the soil in extreme Southwestern Ohio, oddly enough near a farming community also called Palestine.

It was in Ohio that Leah started a permanent attachment to livestock by showing rabbits, sheep, and calves at community fairs.

In later years she supported her college tuition by working on a dairy farm. While some of her high school friends studied to be teachers, Ms. Kloppenstein was intent to take whatever practical knowledge she learned back to the farm.

"I often wondered myself why I chose to concentrate on sows and cows, although some of my friends wanted to teach and become lawyers," said Leah. "I think it might be in knowing that kids will always sass and talk back to their teacher. But cows and pigs don't talk back and they can help buy the farm," she quipped.

Ms. Kloppenstein said her heavy involvement in raising feeder pigs came about through fate. When her son Chris was only three, she stopped by a stock pen to buy him a cute little pig for a pet. As it turned out, the persistent salesman had more ambitious plans fir her.

"He kept insisting that for just a little more money I could own his entire 40 head. Hoping he would shut up, I casually told him I couldn't possibly come up with more than a thousand dollars.

"The next thing I knew, I had committed for the 40 pigs. So, with my life savings tied up into swine, I concentrated on building a profitable business for the future."

Regardless of fate, she has proceeded to make the best of the situation and build a reputation for smart salesmanship along the way. Though content to have one of the county's smaller feeder pig operations, she's careful to avoid pitfalls.

While Leah easily has the space potential to increase both her sow and dairy potential by considerable proportions, she has a firm resolve not to get head over heels in debt.

Fiscally conservative in the ways of old-time Palestine farmers like Joe Looney and Gus Barfield, she is resolved never to invest in new land or expensive equipment unless she is able to pay at least 85 to 90 percent money up front. She knows also that high interest rates, which she compares with the sword of Democles hanging over farmers' heads, can be disruptive to goals.

As with her small sow operation, Leah strives for quality in milk cows. Her favorite is the Brown Swiss which is known for its high proteins and butterfat. Unfortunately, the breed is also a hit with rich hobby farmers who invest heavily in the stock for purposes of grooming at fairs and international shows. That not only makes the cow harder to find, but also more expensive. Nevertheless, Leah — in her zeal to place quality above quantity — has no qualms about climbing into her compact car and driving to distant states such as Pennsylvania to chase promising leads.

While farming is her chosen occupation, Leah's skills for computers and bookkeeping earned her the position of recorder for the City of Henry a couple of years ago. Though happy to practice some of her college earned talents, she found that farming is too confined for moonlighting. Much to the disappointment of former Mayor Wes Archer and present Mayor Tony Brown, she was forced to resign. However, Brown managed to talk her into becoming a fill in for her mother, Karen Kloppenstein, whom the Board of Mayor and Aldermen appointed to take her place.

Leah's reasons for taking on the awesome responsibilities to farm go beyond her love for livestock and hay. It is Chris, her nine year old son. While many single parents frequently turn their children over to a baby-sitter, Leah sacrificed a less demanding career to have the opportunity to stay home with Chris.

You could say that because Leah is so proud of her farm upbringing and all its hard work and rewards, she wants her son to share in that same sentiments.

"I don't hold it against other mothers for hiring baby-sitters to watch their kids so they can go dining or dancing in their free time. But my spare time is so rare and Chris is away so much at school — I feel it a privilege to stay at home with him in evenings."

Leah said she is better off for having learned self-discipline and an appreciation of respect for others in having grown up on a farm. She feels that too many kids are spoiled by modern luxury ... that so many boys her son's age are being permanently scarred by too much television and not any chores.

"Boys get to lying around watching TV, and if they don't have a remote to switch channels as they sit in a cushioned chair, they throw a tantrum.

"My son is being raised in an environment where work comes first and I think he'll become a much better man for it," she said.

This doesn't mean that she professes to put farming before education as was true in the pre-World War II era here, when schools were forced to close for six weeks during cotton picking.

"I am going to see that my son gets the best possible education … that he studies hard and respects his teachers," she said. "I am ready to put off much needed work around the farm in order to see that Chris is progressing properly.

"I know that he's interested in playing football and I will become his greatest fan. I'll get much more involved in taking him to practice and games," she asserted.

Leah, who is close to earning a college degree in finance and management, also is quick to voice the good mother's concerns when she feels things aren't quite right at school.

"I was shocked when I heard that some students at Henry School had asked their teachers where vegetables come from. If we've come to where people believe peas and carrots grow on trees, we're in a world of trouble."

Proud of her family's farming past, Leah would love to see Chris continue the tradition. But she's also a realist and has sadly experienced the decline in small family farms.

"My land is also Chris' land and someday, he'll be in the role of calling the shots. Sure, I'd be happy to see him carry on the family tradition, even if he only rents the farm to other farmers. That would still be income and it would still be family land.

"But if Chris should sell the land, there will still be something valuable that he can't sell at any price. That is the values and self-respect he learned because he was fortunate to grow up on the farm."

Louise P. Brown ...
Mom Cat of Loretto

The Loretta Telephone Company isn't just another means for exchange of communication, it's the heart and soul of the small Lawrence County community. Not only that, but personable owner Louise P. Brown — dubbed "Mom Cat" — is the chamber of commerce for the 2,000 people who live there.

Through the years, the company has grown from a crude switchboard in an upstairs room in the home of William H. Wiggerman to a computerized, modern system serving several thousand customers in Southern Lawrence County communities.

Louise recalls that the first telephone was in Sebastin Dischler's store. "From this wooden box with a mouthpiece, receiver and crank, you could ring "Central," the operator at Mr. Wiggerman's switchboard.

"Central was like an information bureau ... the town's newspaper. You could get the time of day, find out who was sick or had been born , married or died," she recalled.

She remembered that many of the early "Centrals" were some of the Wiggerman girls, like Rose, Minnie and Emma.

A telephone cost twenty-five cents to connect and a user fee of one dollar a month. Since there were no directories, subscribers kept their friends and relatives' numbers in memory or penciled lists.

Each customer had his own rung, a variation on two long and one short, for example, three rings or four and one-half. Eavesdropping was almost regarded as sacred in that it was a source of information firsthand.

Actually, Mrs. Brown's fascination with the telephone began as a child. Once, she talked her mother into taking her to see the old magneto switchboard at the home of her best friend, Bennie Ruth Williams. Bennie's parents then operated the telephone switchboard from their home.

After returning home, Louise, in all her fiery childhood imagination, invented her own "play" switchboard by poking pencils in cardboard and pretending to make the telephone ring.

Her friendship with Bennie Ruth gave Louise the opportunity to be in charge of the switchboard on Sundays while the Williams family attended church.

"I was so excited, my lifetime dream was to operate a telephone switch-board and suddenly it became real," said Mom Cat.

She also found out the immense responsibility involved ... the difference between life and death. The operator of an old time switchboard was regarded as the most important person in the community.

Louise recalled one day when a man died on his job site. She had to immediately notify the priest, an undertaker, and close relatives about the tragedy.

After her marriage to Passarella, the couple moved to New York where her husband worked. In 1946 she learned that Bennie Ruth planned to sell the telephone company she inherited. Mom Cat quickly talked her husband into helping raise $3,600 to buy the business and move to Loretta and become her business partner.

Her dream nearly was destroyed early the following year when a severe ice storm knocked down dozens of telephone poles. Only the quick response of the community which regarded the telephone service as vital to their lives enabled the struggling couple to survive.

"Our friends were generous and understanding. They donated money so that the system could rebuild," remembered Mom Cat.

But as Louise started to bear babies, the pressure intensified. Ralph did odd jobs and worked at the local theater while Louise was at home on the switchboard.

Fortunately, Ruth Reeves — a recent graduate of Loretta High School — applied for a job. So began a close 45-year work relationship, as Ruth not only worked long hours on the switchboard, but helped Mom Cat with the kids.

Ralph was indeed the key man at a critical time. In charge of operations, his remarkable strength was the envy of passing citizens who gasped as he set a telephone pole single-handedly by resting it on his shoulder and then dropped it in the hole.

After the unexpected death of Passarella in 1969, Mom Cat not only faced the problem of running the town's most important enterprise alone, but also was left with seven children to care for.

In 1974, she married Sayles Brown and added four new stepchildren to the family. It was then that she acquired the name Mom Cat.

Likely, Louise — long active in the Democratic Party — would win a race for mayor. But that would be unfortunate for Loretta, even though she would no doubt be well qualified. If she were mayor, the town simply would not have a Mom Cat to keep the people entertained.

As the head of a non profit group called Operation Uplift, the community is always being treated to yearly special events. As its Tennessee Bicentennial project, Mom Cat and her uplift committee organized historical plays which were performed before the public.

Mom Cat sees that Loretta and surrounding communities like St. Joseph, Iron City and Leoma, go all out to celebrate annual Octoberfest. Lawrence County has some quaint German settlements in the Loretta area and Mom Cat makes sure that pride takes center stage.

As a matter of fact, one of her favorite memorabilia pieces near her office desk is a plaque honoring Mom Cat as Burgermeister of an Octoberfest a few years ago.

Mom Cat has enough old time political savvy, learned from her favorite governors, Frank Clement and Ned Ray McWherter, to know that people soon are burned out on the "same old same old". Although a Democrat, Louise knows that in a true two-party system, the spoils come from knowing how to deal with two parties. For instance, she was sad that her good friend, former Congressman Jim Cooper, a Southern Democrat, was defeated by Fred Thompson for a U.S. Senate seat.

On the other hand, the victor was Fred Thompson, a conservative Republican and respected Lawrenceburg native. You can bet that Sen. Thompson, who is heading the investigations into the scandal riddled investigations of the President Bill Clinton administration, and Mom Cat are cordial.

In fact, Mom Cat also relates to Republican Congressman Van Hilliary, who won Cooper's old Fourth District congressional seat.

That kind of nonpartisan political thinking, has not stalled the good express train in Loretta.

In all actuality, the annual festivals in Loretta usually are of short duration. You could safely bet your savings that once the crowds start to thin out, Mom Cat is calling her Operation Uplift to general quarters.

Not too many years ago, the committee organized a Memorial Day parade in honor of the community's war veterans. As usual, Mom Cat bantered nearly 100 percent enthusiasm. As a result of that fever, people in the thousands turned out in a patriotic setting to the town of 2,000 population. In contrast, barely a dozen people were present for a dedication honoring service men who paid the full price, in Paris, Tennessee — pop. 9,300 — the same day.

Not lost in Operation Uplift's zeal to make a difference to the community are such contributions to the city as a gazebo on the square, new street lights, restoration of old downtown buildings and ball fields for the youth.

That community pride also is institution in Loretta High School, at a time of galloping consolidation that has robbed hundreds of Tennessee communities of their high schools and even graded schools.

By and far, Operation Uplift raises its own funds for its many community endeavors. At the same time, Louise uses her immense political connections to get government grants which fulfill some of the greatest town needs.

Mom Cat is likely to say in a course of conversation, that "if you lose the community, you lose (period)."

Her living legacy though, is the Ralph J. Passarella Museum located in two of the town's oldest buildings on Main Street. The museum, through it's hundreds of rare artifacts, relives the fascinating history of Lawrence County. Mom Cat established the museum in 1992 and named it in memory of her first husband.

Jean Willis, museum curator, opens the museum every Wednesday from 1-4 p.m. and will open the facility any time for special tours. Admission is free, but donations are welcome and are used toward upgrading the collection.

Among other things, the Passarella Museum has rare old newspapers, books, toys, tools, quilts, medical equipment, and, of course, antique battery telephones.

From a small four-room house where the Passarellas lived, the Loretta Telephone Company has settled into a large modern brick building near the old depot on bustling Tennessee Southern Railroad. It has also become one of the community's leading employers.

If you ever venture down Highway 43 South between Lawrenceburg and Florence, South Carolina, stop and chat with Mom Cat. It's guaranteed that you'll leave in a better frame of mind.

Progress Can't Get Rid of
Lyin' Good Ole Boys

A ll the theme parks that Dolly Parton can bring to the hills and all the hotels that Kenneth Seaton will build in his lifetime can't exterminate the liars tables of Sevier County.

Take Allison's for example. When booming Pigeon Forge decided to annex north, the owner determined that it was much healthier to join the rush for the mighty tourist dollar than try to get rich selling endless cups of coffee to hillbilly liars for only a quarter.

Undaunted and more stubborn than ever, liars like J. Roy Miller, K.O. McMahan and Carl Hatcher, moved on to more friendly pastures like Minyard Hurst's Cafe in Sevierville. Johnson's, another notorious liars table, was only one door away from Minyard's, so when Jack Connor, Al Smith , Phil Wynn, Albert Atchley or other liars got mad, they'd simply walk their addiction over to Minyard's liars table.

If the truth were known, some of the most earth-shaking land transactions ever had their origin at liars tables at Allison's and Johnson's. For sure, Carl "Big Daddy" Smith, Dayne and Earl LaFollette and Mindle Collier found the way to high cotton while sipping a cheap drink of coffee.

For a fact, you could get a bargain at the liars table, but on a bad day, you could lose your shirt, too. I bought a 17-jewel off brand wrist watch from Delmer Shular at Johnson's back in 1976. It still keeps perfect time, but I can't count the many times I've bought things I didn't need, such as Rotary Club raffle tickets, just to be a good ole boy.

Sometimes, a fellow could really get burned. There was the time some big Orange fan like Jim Ogle bet $500 on Tennessee when they played Army over at Neyland Stadium. The fellow probably would have never taken the bet without the six points to boot.

Army won the game by seven and left one sad Sevierville coffee drunk moaning the blues.

The liars crowd also contributed to the civic end. The brainstorm for the first Sevierville Kiwanis Club had its beginning at Johnson's. The Pigeon Forge Optimist Club had a similar beginning.

Granted, there were a lot of straight deals around the coffee drinking parlors in Sevier County. That doesn't mean every transaction was exactly above board. The late Dick McNabb told me once that he saw the notorious big time drug kingpin, John Ruppel, come into the White Kitchen once with a suitcase. Ruppel whose corrupt drug money built the big castle in Gatlinburg, handed out $150,000 of laundered cash to a land owner for a hideaway farm in some holler near Sevierville.

Who can forget the daily games called liars poker, which were played at Johnson's? I guess Sam Hodges, Carl Hatcher and Fred Hillis were just about the best. It always amazed me the way they could put on that old 'look at my serious kisser' jazz and clean the table.

Gatlinburg had its share of liars tables, that's for sure. Folks like Zeno Wall, Clell Ogle and the twins, Ralph and Roy Maples, can't forget the day a foreigner from up north was sicced on the late arriving Earl Washington Ogle, the postmaster.

The Maples twins, always up to something, tricked the Yankee into posing as a federal postal inspector and telling Ogle he was about to be audited. They say Ogle uttered a couple of favorite mountain cuss words and told the embarrassed Yankee where he could go, conveniently back where he came from.

The old War Bonnet restaurant on Highway 73 East was a throwback to the days when Gatlinburg was still a simple hillbilly haven in the mountains.

That was when hard working folks like Sherill Bradley, Bud Parton, June Ogle, and Pless Profitt had to put up with Sevierville intruders like Dave Johnson and Doug McCarter.

Pigeon Forge had its share of the old time liars tables. There was the famous Corner Cafe & Texaco in old Pigeon Forge. Clyde Seagle, Harold Butler, English McCarter and Bill Maples used to shoot the breeze and talk about trout fishing over on Tellico River.

Trotter's Restaurant near the Spur was popular for the good ole boys too. One reason was its excellent home cooked biscuits.

Z. Buda, the father of the outlet malls in Sevier County, liked the round tables at Hearthside, Apple Tree and Green Valley Inns. Z. and his sidekick, Dr.

St. John, also liked to rub it in when Alabama beat Tennessee in football, which was usually always.

The Big Orange lovers got back though when the Vols finally won. St. John's red door to his office was painted orange by nightriders.

There were other liars tables where a hillbilly could find the time of day, the scores of last night's softball games and what Gladys Breeden was having for dinner at Wilhite.

The coffee drink craze blossomed toward East Gate, when County Commissioner Dana Ogle opened the Corner Market in Frog Alley, but Harold Chance kept out the more sophisticated liars from Sevierville.

Hatcher's Grocery and Restaurant on Wears Valley Road was popular with the folks in Wears Valley and Waldens Creek. County Commissioners Ben Clabo and Riley King usually stopped by to check on constituents. Archie Hatcher was a fixture and now and then, one of Sevier County's few Democrats — like Harold Clabough or Marshall Fox — sat among the liars.

Clabough later opened his own liars table back toward Pigeon Forge. By then the hillbilly had struck it rich as the city of Pigeon Forge started annexation out in the valley.

A fellow could always learn the latest about county politics at George Headrick's City Park Market or Dana's Place in Catons Chapel. That was because County Commissioner Warren Hurst seemed to be everywhere at once.

Politics at the liars tables was awesome ... just awesome. In 1982, I stopped at Ellison's and learned that Wib Ogle was ahead by a thousand votes in the sheriff's race. But when I got to Dixon's Drive-in at Seymour, Carman Townsend had the lead by fifty votes.

If a fellow was really hungry, election time was when you let it all hang out. I remember one year I went to liars tables in Catons Chapel, Sevierville, and Seymour and ate heavily off politicians Frank Allen, Glenn Whaley, and Bat Gibson.

Today, in Sevierville at least, the good ole boys like to solve all the world's problems at Papa Kent's on Dolly Parton Parkway. Many who gather at the liars table every morning are castoffs from the glory days of Johnson's, Allison's and Newman's Cafe.

Herb Lawson, Kenny and T. Rollins, and Jack Thurman frequented Newman's. After Alf Newman sold the cafe just off the courtsquare, they said it just wasn't their kind of atmosphere.

John Ellis, Greely Banks, John Cagle, and Jack Conner had been fiercely loyal to Johnson's liars table.

Then, the great white city fathers succumbed to the Wal-Mart gold and built a traffic island, which was convenient for Wal-Mart, but caused Johnson's to close its doors. The good ole boys had to look for another home.

Not that the good ole boys at the liars tables are likely to appear on the Saturday Grand Ole Opry Show. But I don't think the ole boys get properly recognized for their genuine showmanship. I've seen tourists spellbound after listening to the drawls and watching the artful expressions of mountain folks like Minyard Hurst, J. Roy Miller, Riley King, and Jack Conner. Believe me, I've seen those Yankee tourist eat it up. And just think, it doesn't cost them a dime.

I was sitting at the liars table at Johnson's once when Conner and Glenn King had the floor. I heard this elderly Yankee woman telling her husband ... "To think that we spent $100 for entertainment in Gatlinburg yesterday and here we get the real works for free."

Marshall Hunt ...
Henry County's Road Pioneer

I f any man in Henry County de served the office of road supervisor, it was Marshall Hunt. After all, he served as a faithful apprentice for years, when the safest mode of transportation was the horse and buggy, and the shovel was the laborer's best friend.

Hunt's decision to spend his adult years in the drudgery of a strong-back, barely-paid county road employee, stemmed from his boyhood years grow- ing up on his father's farm in the Possum Trot community of extreme northwest Henry County.

He was only 21 and still much the country boy when, in 1927, his father decided to quit the rural farm life carried on by early generations of Henry County Hunts.

When he moved in with his family at a small house on what is now Brown Street in south Paris, he had his first satisfaction of reading under the luxury of an electric light.

Well ... with some reservations. "We was still about halfway being country folks, because we still had to use the outdoor privy out back," Hunt recalled.

That same year he asked Road Supervisor Marcus Alexander for a job. He quickly found out that picking cotton and suckering dark-fired tobacco was actually easier than clearing brush with an axe and shoveling gravel to build a new road.

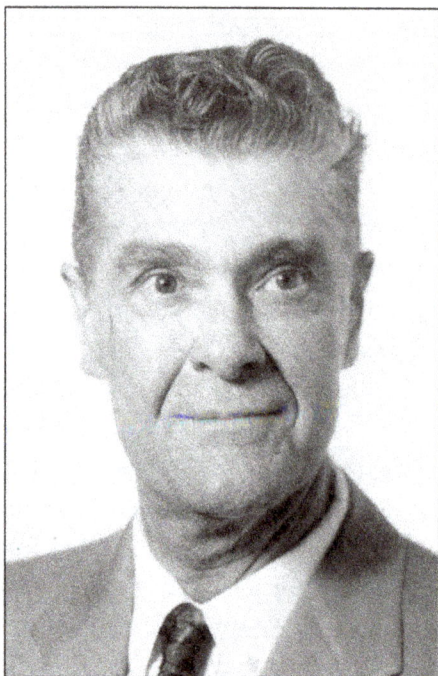

To say Hunt never forgot his raisings is emphasized by his desire to built better roads in the rural areas. As Marshall has said so many times, in the twilight life of retirement, "It was a whole lot safer then to drive to Cottage Grove or Mansfield by horse and buggy than Model T Ford."

During the worst of the Great Depression, Hunt worked for as little as eight dollars a month, but considered it lucky to work at all.

He recalls that the stock market crash of 1929 was not the worst that happened. "From 1930-1933, we had to work in two shifts of three days a week. That was so that everyone had some work and could at least buy bread for the family."

Paved roads might have been culture in Chicago or Memphis, but Hunt said that the best feeling for Henry County farmers was just getting their kids within five miles of school by motor transportation before they had to walk the rest of the way,

He remembers that throughout the 1940s and on into the 1950s, some important roads were still dirt and impassible in cold rainy seasons, other than by horse or wagon team.

It wasn't until after the end of World War II that the county begin to totally fall in with the automobile age.

"We began to see some real progress when Pete Bowles — he was supervisor — talked our budget committee into buying a couple of war surplus road graders.

"The big thing here was that for the first time we could think about grading and graveling roads that people could drive on for the whole year."

In 1950, Hunt, who had served as the right arm for so many supervisors, became the last appointed road boss. The county still had no paved roads and a frightening number of dirt roads. Bridges, for the most part, were in deplorable disrepair, too dangerous in too many parts of the county for school buses to cross with children.

Hunt probably became the first supervisor to look to Nashville for payback.

After all, the state by then had passed a sales tax, and farmers from Crossland, in the heart of tobacco country, to cotton growing Manleyville, were helping the state get richer on each trip to the grocery store.

The problem in Henry County was that children continued to walk a long ways to school or even to meet a school bus that had the luxury of gravel roads and safe bridges.

Fortunately for Hunt — and what would prove more fortunate for the rural folks of the county — the road boss had enough savvy in Democratic politics, to talk to the right people in the governor's cabinet.

He enlisted the state's cooperation in replacing some very unsafe wood bridges with concrete structures.

He pressed his haggard road crew into working hours under hot sunshine to chip and tar a few important connector roads. Things started falling in place all at once.

He impressed the usually spendthrift county budget committee to give enough funds to blacktop roads from Como to Cottage Grove and from Jones Mill to Puryear for the first time ever.

Like a Prussian blitzkrieg in early turn of the century European wars, the Hunt road team rolled into Claytontown and paved on to Buchanan. Very soon afterward, the Reynoldsburg and Henry-Mansfield roads had their very first blacktops.

As unreal as it seems, people in 1960 were still getting bogged down in their cars, trying to drive through the deep mud from Mayfield Highway to Whitlock and from Whitlock to busy state Highway 54 near Puryear (now U.S. Highway 641 N.)

Hunt blacktopped all the way from Mayfield Highway over to 54.

By then, the County Court had enacted legislation calling for popular election of supervisors. But who in his right mind would be crazy enough to challenge a popular incumbent who history will probably credit with transforming Henry County from the horse and buggy age to the automobile age?

The big test didn't come until 1958, when the voting population was young enough to take paved roads and modern, concrete bridges for granted. The poor youngsters had no idea of the sweat and hard labor Hunt and road crews had experienced before and after the Depression.

Many of them were attracted to Hunt's opponent, Sheriff Alvis Wall. Wall had been a popular sheriff — a proven vote-getter from the old school.

For reasons still not fully understood, Wall chose to forego a third and very safe term as high sheriff to take on one of Tennessee's most efficient road supervisors.

Hunt has told friends many times since … "I knew I was in the political scrap of my life. Alvis was a fine sheriff and a powerful vote-getter."

Worse still, Wall was a Puryear citizen which meant that Hunt stood to lose his potent base of support in the north end.

Hunt guesses that he may have spent a month's paycheck stopping in once viable country stores, setting the boys up to nickel dopes and hoop cheese 'n crackers.

"I know I bought everybody in Hays Store and John Hill Store a baloney sandwich and dopes for dinner," Hunt recalled once.

"But the worst part of all was in handing out matches to the old folks setting on the benches around court-square. Having a serious opponent was something I weren't used to.

"I remember stopping to shake hands with Cousin Jim Dumas. He cackled like a duck and said, 'Couz — you used to wouldn't give us the time of the day.'

"You only came around to see us at election time, but now that you got yourself a real tough cookie, you actually spent money to buy us matches."

Hunt squeezed ahead of Wall by 350 votes to keep his winning streak. But that election proved his last.

Now 94 and staying at his Paris home with daughter, Jane Hunt Brown, he sometimes dreams about the possibilities.

"Like there would have been no end to what I might have accomplished for my county if I'd had a tenth of the money they give supervisors now."

Moonshiner's Worst Enemy

WB, during his long career as a mountain moonshiner, has been shot at, seen perfectly good stills wrecked by the wrath of revenuers, even eluded deadly rattlesnakes and bears. He loves the life and feels a duty to manufacturer the best shine in the mountains. Many of his regular customers willingly attest to that. That's why they come back for more good mountain dew.

He could be making plenty of money building houses and dealing in prime mountain land. But WB is so fond of the wild rides and the adventures of stilling white whiskey that he's perfectly willing to take the best shot from the federal agents, battle sneaky snakes and wrestle the meanest bear if that creature tries to steal his sugar and meal.

Beyond a doubt, there is only one thing WB is deathly scared of. That's a woman menstruating who walks by his still while white-lightening is still in the cooking stage.

Not that feminist women have demonstrated for equality as whiskey makers. But to prove what veteran moonshiners strongly believe, "A woman menstruating can ruin a whole batch of fresh distilled shine if she touches it or just gets real close before the 'shine is totally ready," claims WB.

WB said he can't for the life of him understand why a woman's period poisons good moonshine even more than acid in a car radiator.

Ironically, the fact hit home with WB during an interval when he was making moonshine "legally" for a tourist attraction not far from his still.

"This lady came meandering by the whiskey I was cooking and I know she was sick, you could smell her. I knowed she was menstruating something awful and I knowed that when she opened my vat, that the moonshine would be as worthless as a tick on my hound dog.

"That woman poisoned in one little second what I had spent over half the day cooking. But that was what the amusement park hired me for ... to give the

Yankee tourist the excitement of watching a real live Tennessee moonshiner cooking real mountain dew.

But except for a woman whose got the rag on poisoning a good batch of 'shine, WB has no qualms at all about moonshining and that covers getting caught and doing time. WB realized long ago that moonshining has penetrated too deep in his blood.

Yet, unlike so many moonshiners all over Tennessee and the rural South, his art is not steeped in family tradition. Except for a brother who has been his business partner, his family thinks moonshine is truly the devil's brew.

His father, for instance, was a hard-working deputy sheriff, dedicated to putting moonshiners out of business. But people who make illegal booze and avoid paying the government due taxes, expect that and not even the low-downest of the dozens of moonshiners in the county had anything less than due respect for WB's daddy.

That is until his law-enforcing daddy made the near fatal mistake of consorting with every 'shiner's hated enemy, the federal revenuer.

"Roy Tubbs thought he was a real revenuer and he was. He was expert with a rifle, scared of nothing and would jump an eight-foot barbed wire fence to bust a still and make an arrest.

"I know what I'm talking about … Roy Tubbs got after me a few times."

But WB's daddy was allowing Tubbs to conceal his car in one of his barns which happened to lead up the creek into a spring-plentiful holler, ideal for stilling mountain dew. That worried WB more than two stretches in the federal pen.

WB warned his father that some moonshiners who had been caught were upset and talking about getting even with the deputy. "I talked to my daddy until I was blue in the face, I told him that some moonshiners would think nothing about burning his barn down and even his house.

"I didn't expect my father to listen, he had too much pride and a lot of guts. But when it dawned on him that mother might get hurt, he broke off the relationship with Mr. Tubbs."

Like the hundreds of other whiskey makers in the mountains, WB is considered home folks … their kind of man. Many of his brushes with the law haven't even involved moonshine. Maybe a friendly fist fight in which WB obviously comes out winner, might be interpreted as assault and battery by the law. And as any good ole mountain boy will, he's done his share of heavy drinking in the taverns around Newport.

Perhaps the best reason that WB can practice his regular job with little interference, is the good quality of his shine, pure, high proof, white, and chartered. Word gets around in the mountains and some of the richest and most stuck-up folks in the mountains are among his best customers.

Big shot bankers and lawyers from Knoxville and Nashville — even lawman — call on him to deliver a gallon to their offices or homes. It's that old American custom about trying to impress friends or good paying clients by giving them real fine sipping whiskey. Good 'shine is especially good bait for making business sales to investors up north, who have been long fascinated with folklore about moonshining and want to see if it's all real.

Actually, WB's most dangerous brush with the law occurred during a time he lived in Florida. He and a friend from his home area were enticed to come to the Central part of the state by a racketeer who learned that none of the crackers in Florida could hold a candle to WB when it came to making white-lightening.

Indeed, the mountain boys from East Tennessee were rolling in high cotton, selling their 'shine for as much as eight dollars a gallon at a time when gasoline was 22-cents a gallon and beer sold for a quarter a bottle.

The problem rose because the man who owned the land rented by WB thought the Tennesseans were growing oranges. "We found a good piece of property hidden in the orange grove and with the middleman finding us buyers, we were in high cotton for awhile," drawled WB.

But all good things came to an end and the end came when the kindly old gentleman who owned the fruit orchard learned the truth about the two Tennessee hillbillies.

"We were at our still one night and I sensed something was wrong when I kept hearing the sound of automobile tires rolling through sand.

"I went to the edge of the grove and I never seen so many law cars in my life. Some big deputies came in the orchard waving flashlights ... yelling, 'we know you moonshiners are in there — come out, your goose is cooked.'"

Even though the hot sandy flats in Florida didn't offer the protection as in his friendly mountain environment, WB and his hired man managed to get away and hurry to the hills. But their identity was known by Florida authorities. The sheriff of Cocke County was notified and the first familiar face to welcome the mountain boy home was Federal Marshall Roy Whaley, an old family friend.

"Mr. Roy told me he had a warrant for both of us ... said he knew all about Florida and the orange grove. I asked the marshall if I couldn't first get me a good drink of Jim Beam I had hid by the spring. Mr. Roy said, 'I can allow that.'

"He asked about my dad whose health was bad and I told him to go in the house, daddy would love to see him. But Mr. Roy was afraid that my daddy wasn't feeling good and said it was time to go to Newport jail.

"He kept asking about the whereabouts of my friend who he had another warrant for. I didn't want to rat on my buddy, but I knew it was only a matter of time and Mr. Roy handed me five dollars so me and my buddy could get a pint of whiskey after making bail."

Since returning back to the mountains, WB was occasionally bothered by sheriffs who thought the easiest road to reelection was to bust stills in the hollers.

WB was always one step ahead and recanted a humorous event when he and a couple of helpers were cornered near their still. "This gung ho of a high sheriff came hollering for me to come out of the holler hands-up. Said he had me for good. We had blacked our faces and hands so as to try and fool the law. The only way out from where I stood was to run straight up the mountain.

"I took off running hard up that mountain, jumping big rocks and knocking down little saplings, but I got away.

"The next day, a fellow moonshiner I knew, said that I had hired the fastest nigger he'd seen in his whole life. He said that nigger ran so fast over the mountain, a race horse couldn't catch him."

Although WB had once again outwitted the law, he never forgave the sheriff. "I had the biggest and most handsome galvanized still in the mountains … the talk of the hills.

"But that damn gung ho high sheriff hitched it to a car and drug it into town. After he got beat next election, I told him to his face one day. 'All you could do was bust up stills, you never caught nobody in yours whole life.'"

And if the truth was known, WB supplied some of the money that beat "that gung ho high sheriff."

Miss Lillie's Chess Pie
Was Real Sweet

In late October of 1984, when I was editor and publisher of the Smoky Mountain Star in Pigeon Forge, a rural correspondent came to my office to submit her weekly column.

The charming lady, Lillie Owens Huskey, was just one of many thousand country ladies who have helped increase the circulation of small weekly newspapers through their honest, down home, folksy columns. Such unselfish volunteers are the backbone of community-oriented publications in the rural South.

"Miss Lillie," as we at the Star were fond of greeting her, was not just another country correspondent, though. A favorite niece was Avie Lee Parton and Avie Lee is the mother of that famous hillbilly gal singer, Dolly Parton.

The fact that Miss Lillie was great aunt to a famous singer did nothing to take away the simple mountain ways that were the mountain lady's legacy. She once told me "I'm just as proud of Dolly now as I was when Dr. (Robert) Thomas came to Lee (Dolly's father) and Avie Lee's house and delivered yet another baby in that little household."

And, other than Miss Lillie bringing her fine down-to-earth news to my office once a week for my viewing, that was about as close as we ever came to talking about Dolly.

To my pleasant surprise, however, Miss Lillie seemed more intrigued about my West Tennessee roots than about her famous niece.

I might offer an interjection at this point that mountain people in East Tennessee don't immediately fall in love with outsiders. And it doesn't really matter whether the outsiders hail from West Tennessee as I did, or from Dr. Thomas's native Pennsylvania.

Indeed, I recall a speech Dr. Thomas gave to the Sevierville Kiwanis Club once. Dolly was merely one of hundreds of mountain babes the doc had brought into the world since coming to Sevier County. But his message to the Kiwanis that day was understandably bitter.

"I have lived in the rural South for fifty years and I have risked my life driving a horse and buggy through pitch black hollers to heed a request from a worried man whose wife was past ready. Those folks have been so kind to me — have given me their last dollars or even food off their table — but they still regard me as a 'furriner.'"

There's a quaint old mountain saying about sizing a stranger up before accepting him into their world. I think it might have taken a few weeks or at least a few of Miss Lillie's folksy columns before the lady sized me up.

Actually, it came down to a recipe … not the one that Miss Lillie included in that particular column which bore the date, Oct. 18, 1984. It happened that my mother was regularly contributing family recipes from Paris in West Tennessee for the Star. Mother thought that mountaineers might be interested in dishes with a west-state accent.

It's no secret that the two sections of the Volunteer State are separated by more than mere miles. East Tennessee is traditionally Republican, a word that often drew the wrath of the typical redneck from the West Tennessee peckerwoods until recent times. Unlike West Tennesseans, mountaineers in Sevier and other counties in Northeast Tennessee remained fiercely loyal to the union in the War for Southern Independence.

Miss Lillie also ascertained that mother's recipe for chess pie was foreign to her end of the state. When I told her chess pie was my favorite dessert she volunteered to make me one. I could hardly wait until the following week. Sure enough, when the lady submitted her next column, she handed me a chess pie.

I couldn't wait — it had been at least two years since I'd eaten any. I cut a large piece and began licking my chops. Then I took a bite … just as quickly I turned my face while complementing my ace mountain correspondent

It was indeed chess pie, but I'm afraid that Miss Lillie forgot to spare the sugar. Not that chess isn't sweet enough, but the lady — bless her heart — must have emptied in the sack. Other than that, the pie was fine.

As she left my office, I heard Miss Lillie tell a reporter: "The editor really liked my first chess pie. I'll have to make him another pretty soon."

Then I started reading her latest column which she called "This, That and Tuther." Her lead paragraph read: "My niece, Avie Lee Parton, had a birthday the 5th of October. Her daughter, Dolly came to visit her. They had a picnic in the woods like little girls."

And oh yes … Miss Lillie I did enjoy the pie. Well, there was all this sugar, but then it's always the thought that counts.

Bobby Jelks, A Great Coach

T he Army draft, gas rationing, no assistants, and very low pay were only a few headaches that high school coaches fretted about during the early 1940s.

To compound that, Bobby Jelks coached six sports and taught a full load of demanding courses such as chemistry, math and biology. Despite that, Jelks' Grove High athletic teams compared with the better teams in Tennessee and West Kentucky.

But even before he found a lasting home in Paris when he was hired away from Lexington High in 1942, the former college football standout had made an impression as one of the Mid-South's premier motivators.

A native of White Bluff, Mississippi, Jelks built championship contenders out of nearby Gleason High and Sallis, Mississippi. Jelks, who starred on the 1936 Union University team which battled heavily favored Ole Miss to a scoreless tie in 1936, had been on Grove's short list for three years before he came.

The administration at Grove was wanting to move up the football ladder. I learned they were interested in me about the time I coached Gleason.

But by the time they got in contact, I had agreed to coach in Mississippi and later at Lexington.

After graduating from Lexie High School in his native state in 1934, Jelks enrolled at Pearl River Community College in Mississippi. He recalls that one of his most memorable occasions was having a hand in Pearl River's 7-6 win over Southern Mississippi, which was a four year school.

After completing his degree at the junior college, Jelks transferred to Union University. There he played under an assistant coach named Paul "Bear" Bryant, who became one of the all time great college coaches before retiring from the University of Alabama.

"Bear was one of Alabama's players, along with (cowboy actor) Johnny Mack Brown, who won the 1935 Rose Bowl. When Bear came to Union to take

the assistant's job, he brought with him five of the best players that I had ever seen," said Jelks.

That same year, Union capped the season by defeating Murray State College 21-7 to clinch the Southern Intercollegiate Athletic Association championship.

Jelks began his storied high school coaching career at Gleason in 1938. I'll never forget the experience at Gleason. When James Logan, the principal, showed me the facilities, I didn't see any football uniforms or equipment.

"I pointed out my concern and he pointed to a pile of old clothes and badly worn shoulder pads piled on the floor. I told him that I couldn't possibly expect my boys to go out on the field with mediocre equipment like that.

"He told me that the school had no money in the budget for uniforms, but said they had some good credit around town. I got the funds and went to Hunt's Sporting Goods in Mayfield and bought 22 uniforms," he said.

Despite the small town rural environment, Jelks quickly learned that certain boosters in the school's program expected competitive football.

"I was taken in more or less by Doc Bell, vice president of the bank. I learned that some of the boosters had reached out and scheduled me two pretty tough teams, Union City and Milan.

"They were tough folks alright, but we battled Union City to the wire, before they scored in the last two minutes and beat us 13-7.

"Then we went over to Milan and lost out 6-0, but we fought Dresden to a 6-6 tie in the Thanksgiving Bowl which was bit."

Perhaps the highlight of Jelks' brief stay at Gleason was when Bolivar High came to town. I remember the bank president came to me. He was real worried and he said 'Bob Jelks, you won't win today, I just saw the Bolivar team get off the bus and they are big monsters."

But Jelks recalled that Gleason which had starting linemen weighing as little as 122 pounds, won going away. "Chester Blakemore ran 50 yards to a touchdown on a quarterback sneak, there was no turning back," he said.

Jelks left Gleason in 1939 to coach two years at Sallis in Mississippi, where he led his squad to a Big Black River conference championship.

Hired away by Lexington, Tennessee High, his one year there, 1941-42, was one of bitter sweet memories. "I was honored that they wanted me to coach, but I was shocked to hear that Jackson High was one of my opponents.

"Jackson was coached by Tury Oman and everybody knew they were one of the most fearsome teams in the South.

As Jelks feared, his Lexington team was in for a long night. Jackson raced to a 21-0 lead by the end of the first quarter. Oman benched his starting team and Lexington advanced to the five yard line. Oman recalled his rested first string and started pushing Lexington the opposite direction.

"They embarrassed us 50-0, but it was evident that Tury was determined we didn't score. After the game, he came over to shake my hand.

"I took his hand and congratulated his team, but I said 'Tury you embarrassed us tonight, but someday it will be payback time.'"

Pay back time came in 1949 when Jelks' West Tennessee champions of the gridiron buried previously undefeated and unscored on Jackson, 33-6.

While the victory was indeed sweet, Jelks was surprised when word leaked out that Oman was going around Jackson, accusing the Grove coach of running up the score.

"When Roger Murray, a Jackson lawyer and brother of (then) Congressman Tom Murray, told me that, I was shell-shocked.

"The truth is that we could have won bigger, but we had starters like Chick and Dan King and J.C. Hamilton on the bench in the last quarter." he said. Jelks' undefeated 1949 team went on to defeat Memphis Central for the West Tennessee championship.

While the '49 squad is ranked as one of the best Grove High teams ever, Jelks fielded other powerhouses in both football and basketball.

His 1946 squad captured the Big Ten Conference title, but technicalities may have cost similar championships for the 1944 and 1945 Blue Devil teams.

Conference rules required that a team had to play five league games to qualify as champion. Because the Big Ten stretched from Paris to Covington, transportation posed a problem. Like most schools, Grove had to depend on parents to furnish transportation.

Strict war time gas rationing limited the distance that athletic teams could travel. In 1944 Grove, paced by stars like Carl Ross Veazey, Vaden Waddy, Bobby Vaughn and David Hurt, finished 4-0. One of it's wins included a 13-0 win over Milan which was unbeaten at the time.

However, because Grove played only four league contests, Milan was declared champion. The following season, Grove handed Humboldt it's only defeat, but again lost out on the technicality.

Jelks also coached the first high school basketball team in Henry County to the state tournament in 1944-45. The Devils cinched the trip by defeating Memphis Southside in a controversial win at the Divisional Tournament played at Humboldt.

Grove won on a last second shot by Stanley Cooper. The shot bounded off the rim but an official ruled that a Southside player had illegally hit the rim. Southside fans threatened to riot, but Grove went on to Nashville and won the state consolation title.

In addition to coaching both boys and girls basketball, the busy Jelks coached track and a boxing program.

His track team won the 1949 conference track championship, but a disqualification probably cost the thinclads the West Tennessee track title. From his very first football team, Jelks recalls that he was blessed with talent and self-disciplined athletes. However, his 1948 squad was sparked by two tailbacks which can be called a coach's dream.

In Chick King, he had a race horse, power runner who Jelks calls "the best still armed runner I've seen in high school or college."

Then there was little Raz Bilbrey, whose dashing, shifty runs, thrilled fans and haunted would be tacklers.

Jelks, whose teams shifted from the Notre Dame box to the Tennessee single wing, depended highly on tailbacks. In 1947, Bilbrey started at tailback and King was an end.

Bilbrey's reputation as a sure major college athlete surfaced on a September night when Grove played Mayfield on the Murray High field ... much to Jelks' chagrin.

Before the game, Jelks was approached by an assistant coach from the University of Kentucky. "I wasn't prepared for what the coach would say."

"He said Coach Jelks, I'd like to talk to Bilbrey ... I have a scholarship for him in my pocket." It completely floored me," said Jelks. "I said, first off Bilbrey is just a junior and you'll get him in trouble and your university too, if you offer him any scholarship tonight."

About four weeks later, Bilbrey sustained a severe knee injury which virtually ended his football playing career.

King of course was moved to tailback and became what a single wing coach cherishes best, a bone crushing runner and timely passer. In addition, King became one of the South's best high school punters.

Although the 1942 squad Jelks inherited from a previous coach was small an inexperienced, the team was further crippled because some of its older players had been drafted into the Army. But he remembers, "they had hearts big as Texas."

The squad, which included athletes like Billy Hall Puckett, Bud Humphreys, Vaden Waddy and Joe Dudley Mann, finished 5-3-1. Perhaps the most memorable moment was when Dyersburg refused to play because Barton Field resembled a creek after several days of driving rain.

"The coach asked us to pay them the $25 contract, they were going home. We had to pay the officials too," he recalled.

Despite Jelk's success and tireless work day - usually 18 hours - he was paid a salary of only $100 a month. He did receive a free apartment at Cavitt Hall on the campus.

He recalls that he considered leaving only once. After his 1946 team won the Big Ten, he was approached by several other schools which offered better salary.

When Jelks approached Peter Lasater, chairman of the school board, he was told the school would match other officers. His salary was raised $50 monthly. Jelks was given a leave of absence in 1943 when he was assigned to a military college training detachment at Union University. He almost didn't reclaim his job after he decided to play professional football.

He joined the Brooklyn Tigers at their Abilene, Texas training camp in August 1944. He made the team and was offered a contract at $190 per week. In the meantime, he received a call from Grove principal, Charles Pitner, urging him to return to Grove.

"I was caught in a quandary ... I did miss Paris and high school coaching.

"I think what brought on my decision not to pursue a pro-football career came when we scrimmaged the Washington Redskins at Texas Tech University in Lubbock.

"I took a horrible physical beating, the likes of which I had never had before."

Jelks said the decision to quit pro football was a piece of cake, compared to resigning from Grove in 1951 to the job of athletic director, football and basketball coach at Union.

Another major decision came two years later when the Union University Board of Trustees opted to drop football. After much soul searching, he decided to enter the insurance field. He returned to Paris and for several years was associated with Equitable Life of New York.

In 1958 he purchased Paris Insurance Agency. Under his management and later that of his son, Bill, the company has been successful.

His love of coaching has been replaced by civic activity. He remains active in First Baptist Church and is an active member of the Lions where he is a 53 year member and the Masonic Lodge and Shrine Club, where he has been a member for 51 years. He is also a member of the Elks Lodge and Paris Country Club.

By no means though did Jelks leave youth coaching. In 1972, he became active in Pop Warner football, along with Howell McCarty, Jesse Muse and other volunteers.

He has also devoted countless hours to Little League baseball, Boy Scouts and other civic activities. His honors include being named Chamber of Commerce Man of the Year. He was inducted into the Pearl River Community College Sports Hall of Fame. Three years ago, Jelks, along with Chick King, became charter inductees into the Henry County Sports Hall of Fame.

www.ingramcontent.com/pod-product-compliance
Lightning Source LLC
Chambersburg PA
CBHW070837100426
42813CB00003B/651

* 9 7 8 1 5 6 3 1 1 3 4 4 4 *